£2

To Mice
with ~~~~~~~

Jack Vander-Roth
28. 10. 85

ICELAND BREAKTHROUGH

as told by Paul Vander-Molen and written by Jack Vander-Molen

The Oxford Illustrated Press
In association with Channel Four Television Company

© Paul Vander-Molen, 1985
Printed in England by J. H. Haynes & Co Limited
ISBN 0 946609 24 1
The Oxford Illustrated Press Limited, Sparkford, Nr Yeovil, Somerset
Distributed in North America by Interbook Inc.,
14895 E. 14th Street, Suite 370, San Leandro, CA 94577 USA

British Library Cataloguing in Publication Data

Vander-Molen, Paul
  Iceland breakthrough.
  1. Kayak touring—Iceland—Jökulsá á Fjöllum
  2. Ultralight aircraft 3. Jökulsá á Fjöllum
  (Iceland)—Description and travel
  I. Title   II. Vander-molen, Jack
  914.91'2   DL396.J6
  ISBN 0-94660-924-1 ·

Library of Congress Catalog Card Number
85–81001

Contents

To Moo and Yarpe and the rest of my family

Acknowledgements

I should like to express my thanks to my family who supported me not only through the preparation and execution of 'Iceland Breakthrough', but through the writing of this account of that expedition. Special thanks go to my father, Jack, who patiently and skilfully wrote this book for me as I dictated notes and stories to him from my hospital bed, and to my brother Leon for his inspired poetry which also appears in this book.

I should also like to express my gratitude to the following companies who so generously donated food, clothing and equipment to 'Iceland Breakthrough' and without whose help the expedition would never have got off the ground:

Ultimate Equipment	Robin J. Sports Ltd
Olis	The Family House
World Wide Films	Honda
BP Oil	Ever Ready
Samuelsons	Spacecoats
Icelandair	Ventile
Alafoss of Iceland	Vickers Medical
Fosters Lager	National Westminster Bank
Peter Cox	Butterdane
Canoeist Magazine	Go Plane
Vacuum Reflex	Southdown Sailwings
Colmans	Twickenham Travel
N.A.O.	Wave Sports
Strobe Indent Ltd	Damart
Avon Inflatables	Victor Summer & Co Ltd
I & M Steiners Ltd	O-Zee Leisure Ltd
Burndept Electronics	66° North
Schwartz Spices	Höfn Co-op
Survival Aids	Silverscreen
Poulloux	Michel Duret
Emery	Trappeur
Prodeal	Bel
Delpeyrat	Gaybo
Fuji Film	Canon
Spenco	SEB
Gales	Free Blades
Béré	Snowcat Hire

My thanks also go to Mick Coyne for his friendship and support throughout; to Tony Escritt for his help in checking the manuscript; to Howard Smith, Hardie Brown and the people at Sabatini Taylor Assocs Ltd, Fred Olsen Travel and Cameron Choat & Partners for their help and advice; and lastly to the team members of 'Iceland Breakthrough' who made the expedition such a memorable event: Mick, Benoit, Jeb, Gerry, Jean-Luc, Robert, Bruno, Jean Jacques, Gísli, Gudbrandur, Simon, Didier, Bruno-B, Marc and Kári.

All photographs reproduced in this book are with the kind permission of Jean-Luc Cheron and Robert Grégoire.

Preparation

The Idea

Down below me I could see the glistening ice with small white flecked peaks and points, occasionally heightened and made feathery by the mountain wind. Above me, cumulus cloud moved slowly across a pale blue sky like giant ragged cotton wool balls. I stood between ice and sky on a cliff's edge high above an Alpine valley. And then I jumped! I jumped over the edge and floated gracefully down in a hang-glider which at first rose and soared and then glided down like an elegant pterodactyl, adroitly controlled by my instructor, for this was my first flight, and at once I experienced the exhilaration of Superman! But then I realised that I was a passenger, the cargo—and the idea came to me—if the hang-glider could carry my weight in addition to the pilot it could easily carry a thirty-two pound kayak in my place, provided it could be fastened in securely.

* * *

I was living in Paris, and thinking about setting up an expedition to cross Greenland using hang-gliders to fly off mountains for reconnaissance ahead of a ground-based team. I went into the Astrolab to look at some maps and by chance I came across one of Iceland. I saw a great glacier and issuing from it a long river with four bars across it—four immense waterfalls. It was called the Jökulsá á Fjöllum (pronounced the Yokulsa-a-Feeotlum) and gradually, Greenland forgotten, the idea of exploring this river became paramount in my mind—but how to do it?

How to overcome the falls? It was then that I had a flash of inspiration—we could use the hang-gliders as planned but with kayaks combined. The idea grew in my mind and as it grew, it changed. A normal hang-glider with kayak attached sounded like an interesting project—but a *powered* flying machine, a microlight, with perhaps *two* kayaks seemed to open up tremendous possibilities, not only as a very flexible mode of transport but also as a very economic method of exploration. The more I thought of it, the more the idea obsessed me.

I wondered whether a microlight could be made to float and if it could take off from water. How would a kayak act in the air and how would a wing work on water? These were the questions to which I had to find answers and as I found them my idea gradually began to emerge from its chrysalis state into a plan, tentative and hesitant at first but then, butterfly-like and beautiful, into an event which was to change my life.

The Plan

Chance plays such a vital part in our lives. It was chance that brought Mick Coyne to the

1982 Canoe Exhibition at Crystal Palace. Mick, an expert and enthusiastic kayakist, was planning a trip to Norway. He approached me for advice, knowing that I had just recently returned from the 'Valley of Ice' expedition on the wild Alsek River in Alaska, where we had taken our kayaks to venture where no man had been before and where, in cruel conditions, we had learnt the danger of challenging nature's wildest elements. I listened for ten minutes and then I told him 'I can't help you!'

'I can't help you—because you've got it all. I would do exactly as you propose to do—it's great!'

But in those ten minutes a friendship arose, and when subsequently Mick phoned me, we arranged to meet in September. His reputation had preceded him and I had learned much of this man who was to become a devoted friend and colleague. Aged 25, a gentle caring giant, 6'3'' tall, he in no way typifies the image of the fighting man and yet, having served five years with one of the toughest Corps in the world (The Royal Marine Commandos), he is in every sense a man of action. A very enthusiastic kayakist, he spends much of his time as an instructor for boys' clubs, and with his compassion for the underprivileged, devotes many hours to the youth of London's East End. He holds a degree in Geography and Ecology. He has a very strong and forthright personality and makes a loyal, staunch friend, being at all times steady, optimistic, and good humoured. An excellent organiser, his preference however, is to be self sufficient, and he does not enjoy delegation. Whilst he is prepared to undergo the most physical of hardships and shows great courage and fortitude in times of danger or stress, he will very cheerfully opt for comfort when occasions offer it—he prefers a hotel to a tent! An all-round sportsman, this tall good-looking man is highly popular with all who meet him, and an excellent choice for companion on an expedition such as Iceland Breakthrough.

When we met in September, I talked of my idea about microlights, kayaks and of Iceland. Mick, game always for excitement and new experiences, had served on a frigate off the Icelandic coast during the so called 'Cod War' and had been fascinated by the volcano and the ice. He agreed—'Iceland it is!' We knew it would be hard—but with the confidence I had gained from my experience in Alaska, my enthusiasm grew. Mick, who during his time as a Royal Marine Commando had added to his skills as a kayakist, those of climbing, skiing and parachuting, was equally excited and we both began to plan our next moves with a will. We would need a pilot. We would need a team. We would need money. Of all these had we none—but we had a dream and we would make it come true.

We knew nothing of Iceland—and so we sought out maps, books and information. Then as we learned more of the subject we talked and talked. On one occasion we talked for over seven hours, about the beautiful long rivers with high waterfalls and crashing icebergs. We talked of the hard volcanic terrain, the isolation, the cold, the glaciers . . . and the more we talked, the more magical it became. We obtained statistics and learned the population count was 224,384 people of whom over 83,000 live in Reykjavík. We had read that of Iceland's 39,750 square miles (103,000 sq km), almost 23,000 square miles (60,000 sq km) were mountains of 1300 feet (400 m) and higher, while glaciers occupied some 7500 square miles (12,000 sq km). Vatnajökull glacier alone is said to occupy a twelfth of Iceland's wild and harsh terrain. The Central Bank of Iceland told us how many inhabitants per doctor, the number of TV sets per 1000 inhabitants, how many cars, telephones and such things. We learned the age of men and women, the

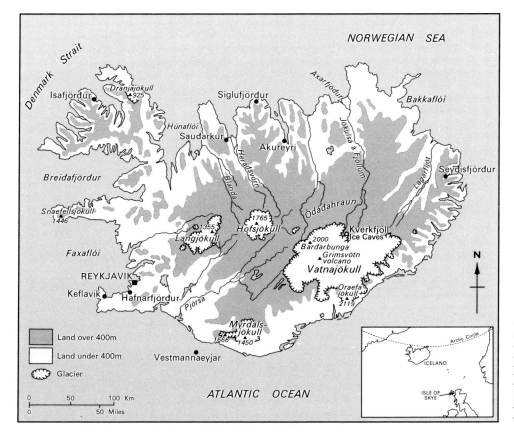

Of Iceland's 103,000 sq km, almost 60,000 sq km are mountains of 400 m and higher, whilst glaciers occupy some 12,000 sq km. The Vatnajökull glacier alone is said to occupy a twelfth of Iceland's harsh terrain.

industrial distribution and the number of foreign visitors.

But they did not tell us of the proud, strong and friendly Icelanders, of their heritage, of the Sagas and the ancient link with Denmark. They did not speak of their generosity, or their cleanliness. *We* learned of their pride that such a small country, so sparsely populated, boasted (we were told) the highest number of new book titles published annually per head of population, a testimony to their thirst for knowledge. We learned from *our* books that in this almost treeless country there are beautiful fertile areas where short, sturdy, multicoloured horses graze contentedly in fields. They are part of Iceland's story and feature strongly in the Sagas, those brooding tales which have been passed down through hundreds of years of firelight talk. The Icelanders are above all a race of poets, inspired perhaps by the nature of the country: the sharp contrast between volcanic lunar landscape, icy mountain, waterfall and torrent, and the gentle rolling fields of the south, with its busy fishing ports; the colourful red and green roofs of Reykjavík and Keflavík. The nature of contrast lends itself to lyrical description—it is a poetic and ancient land.

There is a story, dear to the hearts of Icelanders, about how their country got its name and the founding of their capital city. It begins with some early Viking settlers, led by one Ingólf Arnarson who arrived on the shores close to the place where we would land our expedition, at Jökulsárlón, the Glacier Lake. Tradition has it that the name Iceland stems from the first view these Viking men had of the enormous Vatnajökull glacier—they thought it was truly a 'land of ice'. The year was AD 874. Ingólf was a wise leader—he knew that he would have to settle in various places but that in unexplored territory it would be difficult to make a choice of site. They encamped close to where they had landed, and from his longship, Ingólf took a beam of wood which he had brought across the sea. This wood had been taken from the entrance of a Temple in his homeland. It had been chosen with great care, perhaps for its markings, or perhaps for its unique shape or perhaps even because it would have had some mystic significance in their pagan beliefs. He ceremoniously cast this beam far out to sea saying 'Where this wood comes to rest, there will I build a fine town'. The current carried the wood away from Jökulsárlón and out of his sight, and he waited. Sometime later, he sent out runners to traverse the whole of Iceland in search of the door post. One year elapsed, then two, and then in the third year, one of his emissaries discovered it, washed up on to a gravelly beach, and close to a warm geothermal source. True to his word, he travelled to this place and there set his craftsmen to build a new settlement which grew into a town. This town became Reykjavík—capital of Iceland. And as the wood was brought there by sea, so come all the treasures of Iceland.

The Plan Grows

Over the next few weeks and months a plan gradually emerged. I had decided to work full time on the project and my first efforts were directed towards deciding upon the route we would travel, clarifying our aims, choosing a team, obtaining finance and equipment—and learning to fly a microlight! From our study of the map, we realised that Vatnajökull glacier was en route from the coast to the source of the Jökulsá á Fjöllum River and that we should consider the possibilities of crossing the glacier, rather than making a long trek around it. We studied the maps of Iceland in the Geography Department of City of London Polytechnic where Mick was reading for a Geography Degree and it was here we discussed the feasibility of crossing the mighty Vatnajökull glacier to explore the Jökulsá á Fjöllum River beyond.

If we take the Vatnajökull glacier as a so to speak 'earth mother' we might reflect upon the life emanating from this massive ice cap in two opposite directions; north and south. From her southern fringes she supplies a lake, some three or four miles (5 km) across, with water and some icebergs, many small, but some as large as houses. And then this lake, called Jökulsárlón, closes in and becomes just a small river also called Jökulsá, 1½ miles (1km) long which glides into the sea, through gravel beaches. But in the north, and rising magically from subterranean ice caves, heated by geothermal activity beneath the glacier, speeds the great Jökulsá á Fjöllum, 125 miles (200 km) long, over falls and through canyons, by rapids and serene passes, on its journey to the Arctic Ocean. This was the open ended glacier, upon which we were to try our strength.

As our plan grew, Mick and I agreed that it would make a wonderful start to the journey if we were to cross the sea in a sailing boat, to arrive in Iceland at the same place as the early settlers had landed almost a thousand years ago. And this led us to look at the lake, Jökulsárlón, as a potential starting place for the expedition. We would bring a boat near the entrance to the lake, and from there we would disembark with kayak and raft, and start the journey proper. On the lake we planned to test our equipment, try out

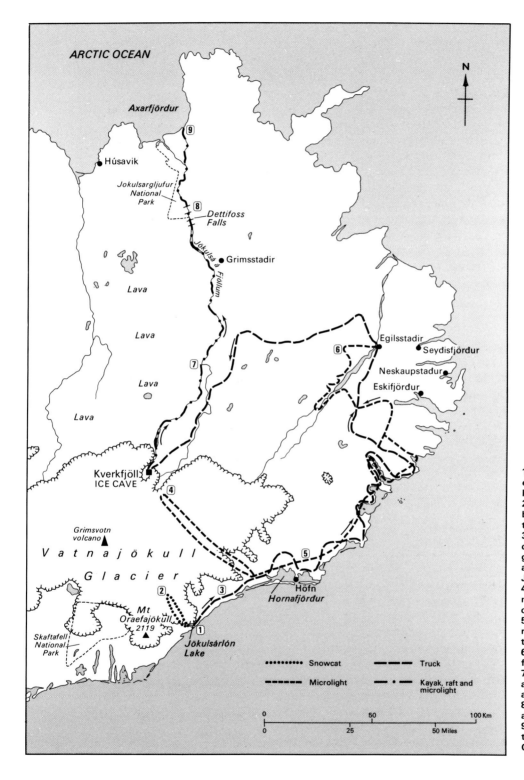

ARCTIC OCEAN

Axarfjördur

N

Húsavik

Jokulsargljufur
National
Park

⑨

⑧ Dettifoss
Falls

Grimsstadir

Lava

Lava

Lava

⑦

Egilsstadir

⑥ Seydisfjördur

Neskaupstadur

Eskifjördur

Lava

Kverkfjöll
ICE CAVE

④

Grimsvotn
volcano ▲

V a t n a j ö k u l l

G l a c i e r

⑤

Höfn
Hornafjördur

②

③

Mt
Oraefajökull
2119 ▲

Skaftafell
National
Park

①

Jökulsárlón
Lake

•••••••••• Snowcat   – – – – – Truck

– – – – Microlight   – • – • – Kayak, raft and
                                      microlight

0 _____ 50 _____ 100 Km

0 ___ 25 ___ 50 Miles

1. **July 26th 1983,
expedition arrives from
Isle of Skye.**
2. **Weather halts attempt
by Snowcat and whole
team to cross the glacier.**
3. **The surface team
detours around the
glacier to the Ice Caves
and the source of the
Jökulsá á Fjöllum river.**
4. **Weather halts
microlight attempt to
cross the glacier.**
5. **Microlight follows
route of vehicles around
the glacier.**
6. **Crash landing due to
faulty exhaust.**
7. **Repaired microlight
and second microlight
arrive.**
8. **Crew and equipment
airlifted over waterfalls.**
9. **After six weeks, the
team reach the Arctic
Ocean.**

the cameras and sound recorders, fly the microlights, and acclimatise ourselves to the cold.

After the lake, six of us would ski across the glacier, using a Snowcat (like a huge snow tractor) as a mobile base. We planned to scale the great mountain Oraefajökull, lying south on the glacier, and to the west of the lake, and after this we would continue on to Grímsvötn Volcano where we would meet up with the rest of the team. (Grímsvötn, an active volcano, actually erupted seven weeks before the start of the expedition—we thought we would be prevented from going and might have to cancel the whole project! This catastrophe, just when we were in the last stages of putting our expedition together, was one of the most unkind acts of fate—our sponsorship programme was affected, and if our enthusiasm for the venture had not been so great, our determination would have been sadly eroded. We kept hoping that it would be all right, and anxiously studied every report we could get of the area. Gradually it became apparent that we *would* be able to proceed, even if we had to slightly modify our plans.)

The Snowcat would then return to the lake while the rest of us made our way to Kverkfjöll in the north, on skis and skiddoos, towing our kayaks. At Kverkfjöll we would find the ice caves. Strange holes appear in the glacier's surface some distance from its edge, and these link up with caves formed at the point where the river flows out of the glacier. We would enter these caves if we could, and attempt to kayak down the Jökulsá á Fjöllum from beneath the ice—at the river's very source.

For our journey proper, the navigation of the river from source to sea, we would require 4 kayaks, 2 rafts for carrying supplies, and 2 microlights to carry men and equipment over the waterfalls and any other impossible terrain we might encounter. We would also use the microlights to scout ahead—a simple but quite unique concept, and one destined to open up a completely new field of endeavour in the exploration of our planet. The microlights could be adapted to carry kayaks, and in turn could be stripped down to a manageable size and shape and be carried by the rafts, our 'inflatable aircraft carriers', when not required to fly. We would thus have great flexibility in our mode of travel.

The River

The river almost chose itself. Once I had seen the map, I could not resist the challenge of those mighty falls, and once Iceland had become the focus of my attention, I saw that there were two major rivers emerging from the Vatnajökull Ice Cap, and from my experience of rivers and glaciers in Alaska, I found it rather easier to 'read' than a 'rain' river. When a river derived from a glacier, I could assess its flow rate and whether it would be big enough for a large expedition. I knew that it would have ice—and then as soon as I saw the waterfalls, that for me was it! I had this strange feeling that once I had made a decision, bonuses would be added to it. It happened in Alaska and I was sure it was going to happen here in Iceland as well. There would be lots of things going on around it, which could enhance our venture. The idea of taking the microlights and kayaks over the falls gave us the certain feeling that this would become *our* river.

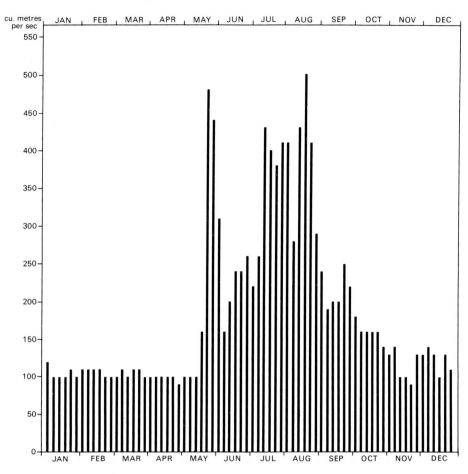

For Iceland Breakthrough,
Paul and Mick studied
forty years of flow charts
so as to estimate the peak
flow dates.

To understand Jökulsá á Fjöllum, it is necessary to look at the geology of the area. Iceland is situated upon a mid Atlantic Ridge formed by two moving tectonic plates under the surface of the ocean. It is a highly volcanic area, and I cannot better the description given in a recent geological survey, a précis of which follows.

The river is situated in the eastern part of Northern Iceland, originating in the glacier Vatnajökull and flowing towards north in a broad arch to the town of Axarfjördur. One hundred and twenty-five miles (206 km) long, it is the second longest river in Iceland (Thyórsá being longer). At the headwaters lies the great glacier Vatnajökull. Here at the source, the elevation is about 2500 feet (750 m) compared with about 800 feet (250 m) at the mouth near Axarfjördur. The surrounding mountains rise up to 3000 feet (1000 m) above the plateau.

On its journey north the river has cut a canyon in the rock. The name of the canyon is

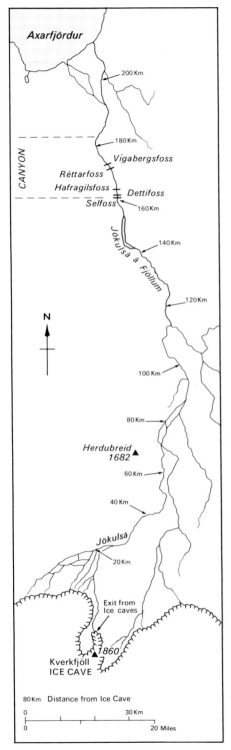

Jökulsárgljúfur, and it extends from the waterfall Selfoss to slightly north of the farm called Vestaraland, where the river then flows out on to the sandy plain of Axarfjördur-Kelduhvervi. The canyon measures 20 miles (30 km) in length, and shows many beautiful rock formations, mainly of columnar lava. The mighty falls of glacier water, made brown by suspended volcanic ash, contrast with the clear blue water issuing from the many springs on the nearby slopes, and the sharp rocky and rugged appearance of the canyon is highlighted by comparison with nearby sheltered spots of luxuriant vegetation as at Hólmatungur, and Forvöd. The scenery is magnificent.

The canyon naturally divides itself into three portions. In the north, extending about 8 miles (11 km) it is late post glacial, mainly eroded during the last 2500 years. The middle section, some 5 miles (9 km) long is roughly a U-shaped valley with boulder and gravel terraces at different heights. It is partly formed by glacier erosion, but the present bed of the river on its bottom is in some places cut down to bedrock forming a second canyon. Near the upper end of this section are two waterfalls, Réttafoss and Vígabergsfoss. The southern-most section, about 6 miles (9.5 km) long, is formed by backward erosion of a series of waterfalls. It is the deepest part of the canyon and it is here that Hafragilsfoss 90 feet (27m) high, Dettifoss 145 feet (44m) high, and Selfoss 35 feet (11m) high, are situated. Dettifoss is the mightiest waterfall in the whole of Europe, from whose rocky height there cascades each second, more than 17,500 cubic feet (500 cu m) of water.

South of Selfoss there are turbulent rapids and then the river sometimes quietly, sometimes with savage fury, drives itself the remaining 60 miles (100 km) to the sea.

In the years 1490, 1655, 1684, 1711, 1716, 1717, 1726 and 1729 to name but a few, there was recorded a *Jökulhlaup*, which is Icelandic for a glacier burst. The one in August 1729, was caused by volcanic activity beneath the Vatnajökull. Heat gradually began to melt the ice. A water pocket containing millions of tons of water and ice burst, actually lifting the glacier. The result was catastrophic. A flood covered an immense area, killing off wild life. Even birds succumbed to the noxious sulphuric fumes of the water. Smaller floods have been recorded at least ten times each century—roughly every ten years and it was nought for our comfort to learn that the last glacier burst had been in 1972.

Under the ice cap, volcanoes lie hidden, hot water sources boil, and the 'dead' area 'lives'. The ice is blue—and cold. The water is strangely warm—a magical subterranean land of smooth, melted ice walls and steaming rivulets. And from here the Jökulsá á Fjöllum finds its way to the light, cuts its way through the lava, and falls in mighty gushes to the canyon, on its continuing journey to the Arctic Ocean.

The description of ice caps, volcanoes, caves, boiling water, immense waterfalls and the pictures of Iceland's rugged grandeur, awe-inspiring in its challenge, fired our enthusiasm to explore its mysteries.

At this stage in our planning Mick and I realised that before we could proceed any further with our scheme, we would need to find a pilot. This was absolutely essential for while both Mick and I were willing and eager to learn to fly, we realised that we would need a pilot of exceptional ability to enter into this new realm of exploration. When I was working in Paris, I had decided to go to the Bois de Boulogne to see the first arrivals of the very first London to Paris Microlight Race. I obtained a press pass and was immediately transported into a scene from *Those Magnificent Men In Their Flying Machines*. The first man to land wore World War II flying gear and I rushed over to congratulate him in my best French. 'Sorry mate—don't understand a word!' said Gerry Breen, aviator extraordinary, holder of five world records and a man of adventurous spirit. At that time I asked him if he would be interested in an expedition, and subsequently we had some talks about my ideas. He rather thought I was pulling his leg—microlights, kayaks, waterfalls? His record and reputation were all we needed to be totally convinced that he was the man for us and so we approached him formally about joining our venture. On the other hand *he* was not convinced *we* were the men for him—we were 'crazy' and in his book that really means 'gone'. But he did join us, and when later I talk about our team I shall try to do justice to this high flyer.

At the same time we needed to know a lot more about our proposed destination. I made enquiries about Iceland from various sources and found that all roads led to Tony Escritt. He takes up the story of our first interview, in his own words.

'A young man by the name of Paul Vander-Molen called me to see if he could come in to talk about Iceland. He was thinking of canoeing down the Jökulsá á Fjöllum. I didn't say anything but thought that it was a good job that he was coming to see me. When would he like to come? "In about 20 minutes", he replied. "The fellow's in a hurry," I thought.

'In the meantime one of my geographer colleagues came in to see me. I forewarned him of the visit thinking he might be of use in our meeting and then rang Nigel Winser at the Royal Geographical Society just to see if he knew anything about this one. "Oh, Paul? Yes, he's one of our most experienced white-water canoeists." I didn't need to hear any more.

'The bell rang, and this energetic, folder-laden young man bounded up the stairs, and extended a large friendly handshake (more of a paddle squeeze). He bore down the passage like a rising tide, assuring me that he wouldn't keep me. Scrapbooks, folders and maps proceeded to be unfurled on the dining room table. Page by page he rushed through previous exploits, mindboggling in their audacity. I could see that my colleague was becoming increasingly uncomfortable. I hardly had time to say more than a "yes" or "no" as Paul rushed through his preliminaries. "We plan to kayak over Dettifoss!"

'My colleague excused himself at this point with a polite but obviously disbelieving smile. I must admit to trying to suppress my horror, but years of assisting way-out expeditions had taught me that nothing is impossible until proved otherwise. "It could be a once-in-a-lifetime experience," I thought.

"It will be an international expedition" said Paul and he reeled off an impressive list of Frenchmen. I wondered if the man was French—something had to explain this lunacy.

"Gerry is building a microlight that will be able to land on skis or wheels and which will carry the kayaks as floats." It was getting worse. Gradually the whole plan was beginning to unfurl. Sailing from the UK, landing on the southern shores, flying over the Vatnajökull, landing on Grímsvötn. "Oh, how big is Grímsvötn lake? Can we land on it do you think?" I had to say that as a rule there really was no lake up in the crater because of the snow and ice. So that one had to be revised. "How high is Dettifoss?" "How fast is the river at that time?" "What sort of weather can we expect in August?" He was laden with innumerable questions, some of which I could provide the answers to, but some of which were so out of the usual line of questioning that I did not have them at my fingertips.

Left: **The Jökulsa á Fjöllum river from source to sea. The source of the river begins at the Kverkfjöll Ice Caves, underneath the Vatnajökull glacier. From there it is shallow and braided until it narrows in the canyon and falls in a thunderous roar over the waterfalls.**

'The whole idea was so preposterous that it just had to be believable. There was no doubt in our minds that Paul was going ahead with this and that his team was about as equally well-qualified in lunacy that if they couldn't do it no one could. So—give 'em the rope. My feelings were echoed by my good friend Hannes Hafstein, director of the Iceland National Lifesaving Society, who later telephoned me after Paul had been to see him on my recommendation. "Tony," he said, "These guys are absolutely mad!" and he spat each word out with great emphasis. "I cannot stop them, the Research Council cannot stop them, no one can stop them. So, what can I do but give them every damned bit of help that I can?" It was a view shared by everybody. These were nice guys, doing a thorough job in preparation, paying attention to every single little detail. They deserved our support and they duly got it. Even the late and great Professor Sigurdur Thórarinsson gave them a couple of hours of his time and that was indeed an honour.

'Two hours later Paul left our home. Not only had we seemingly exhausted all the potential snags but also vexed over what to call the expedition. Jenny had scrawled away at one end of the table and emerged with "Iceland Firefly" [later to be changed to Iceland Breakthrough] and a logo not dissimilar to the eventual cartoon sticker.

'Thereafter, Paul called in to see us at regular intervals and was frequently on the phone to check a detail or to locate a contact in Iceland. In retrospect I must say that his almost boyish enthusiasm and amazing energy carried us both along to the extent that we almost felt a part of the expedition.'

* * *

Reconnaissance I

After the meeting with Tony Escritt, Mick and I went to Iceland. We had a lot of information, we had some people to visit, places to see, and, now that Gerry had agreed to be our microlight pilot, we were full of confidence.

And so we started to open doors. Tony and another friend of ours, Ian Wilton, who at that time worked with a travel firm in Middlesex, had provided us with a long list of people to contact in Iceland, all of whom contributed in full measure to the ultimate realisation of the dream we had started. We first saw Mr. Brian Holt, a retired British Consul. This gentleman was very much of the British Air Force and Diplomat tradition. Though highly sceptical of such a harebrained scheme, he was most kind and helpful. Through him we met Sigurdur Rist, in charge of Iceland's Water/Power Authority. He gave us charts, records and an introduction to the map office where we obtained USA aerial charts and photographs (taken to supplement a plan to dam a river, a scheme which was later aborted). From the weather authorities we obtained weather forecasts.

Chance, as I have said, enters our lives and shapes our destinies. Once again, it intervened. We were walking along a street in Reykjavík when we saw a car approaching with a hang-glider strapped to its roof. I flagged it down and spoke to the driver, who plainly thought we were mad Englishmen! We had coffee and discovered that he, Einar Eríksson, ran a Camping Company called 'Rent-a-Tent'. We learned much from him and were introduced to Kári Gudbjörnsson, a pilot, climber and skier, who as a result of this meeting was later to become a member of the team, as reserve pilot. Tony has told of

Right: **This photograph captures the drama of the Jökulsá canyon and Dettifoss, Europe's highest waterfall. The microlights were invaluable in reconnaissance work.**

the amazed reaction of Hannes Hafstein, a man who was to become a firm friend and supporter and without whose skill, knowledge and influence we would have been hard put to succeed. He found time always to listen to us, to advise, to introduce us to those who could help, and took us under his all-encompassing wing, trying to offer the greatest safety and security consistent with the hazards of our scheme. Not that we always agreed—we did not—but we were all very much on the same side, and that counted for everything as far as we were concerned.

Hannes is a great man, with a great heart—and built to match! I can still recall our meeting. He burst out in hysterical laughter when he heard that we were going to canoe down the river. Complete disbelief! Icelandics do not usually think of rivers to canoe down but as obstacles to cross using vehicles—Hannes Hafstein thought the idea of canoeing down the Jökulsá at all, was crazy. He roared 'Do you know that there is a waterfall down this river, and what, Mr. Vander-Molen and Mr. Coyne are you going to do about this?' in his rich Icelandic English.

Mick and I looked at each other and thought 'Oh God, who's going to tell him?'

When we had first arrived in Iceland we travelled from Keflavík to Reykjavík along a road upon which we noticed there was a complete absence of trees. There are, in fact, very few trees in Iceland, and in some parts there are none at all. Later, after Mick and I had been introduced to Kári Gudbjörnsson and we were enjoying a meal at his house with more friends of his, the conversation turned to our respective careers. They wanted to know what Mick and I did, apart from being explorers. And so we told them. Then we wanted to find out about our fellow guests—one was called Ivar, an engraver, another was Einar of 'Rent-a-Tent', and then we spoke to a pleasant rather chirpy sort of man sitting opposite Mick. 'And what's your line?' asked Mick of this guest.

'I'm in the Forestry Commission,' he said.

Mick and I looked at each other—was he pulling our legs?

'You're in the what?' I asked.

'The Forestry Commission,' he affirmed.

'But there are no trees in Iceland—are there?' asked Mick, 'What do you do?'

By this time we were trying hard not to giggle and offend him and our host.

'Yes—well, I'm in the Commission to try to get some trees growing in Iceland!' Luckily they saw the funny side of it too and no feelings were hurt.

*   *   *

We learned a great deal on our first visit to Iceland. Above all we discovered that the Icelandic people were friendly, open and helpful. Perhaps it was this fact more than any other that made us even more determined to go ahead with our expedition—a venture which had certainly been received with some considerable scepticism. In spite of this, everyone we had met had gone out of their way to help us, and we returned to England laden with papers, charts, data sheets, and above all, good wishes.

We wondered if it would come off, and we worked hard to convert our idea into a practical plan and then into action. And into action we went, Mick, Gerry and I. We realised that we needed publicity and that it was time to formalise our aims into a brochure which we could circulate for potential sponsors and team members. We needed money, men, and equipment, and we set out to get them.

Our Aims

We had four primary aims. They were:

1. To prove that motorised hang-gliders and kayaks can be used together to create a new and powerful exploration technique.

2. To attempt the first ever descent of Jökulsá á Fjöllum from its source within the ice caves beneath Vatnajökull glacier, down to the Arctic Ocean.

3. To film a full record of the expedition.

4. To attempt to cross the Vatnajökull glacier.

We had some secondary aims too, which were:

1. To climb Oraefajökull, the highest mountain in Iceland and to descend by skis and microlights. The mountain is on the glacier.

2. To visit Grímsvötn, an active volcano in the centre of the glacier.

3. To climb the east face of Askja volcano, and to canoe upon the lake within its crater, reputedly one of the deepest volcanic lakes in the world.

4. To explore a 'Ghost River.'

(As the story unfolds it will be seen that for reasons beyond our control, these aims had to modified, but at this planning stage we were fully committed to them.) And so, as we went forward to the task of forming a team, we had a clear idea of the 'shape' of our expedition, and this was tremendously helpful during our meetings with prospective members.

The Team

Choosing the right people to share difficulties and dangers is not easy. On what basis do we act? Should we look first at the skills of the man and then at his compatibility with the rest of the team? Do we go by reputation and recommendation? How far should we be guided by gut reaction? All of these factors came into play, but the over-riding consideration in the selection of our team members was the one of compatibility. Given the skills, we set out to create a team of unity and goodwill.

We needed rafters, kayakists, skiers, pilots, climbers and transport men. It was essential to have a really first-class cameraman for the movie film we planned to make, and an experienced sound recordist. We needed 'still' photographers, and then with the hazards of the expedition in mind, we certainly needed someone with medical skills. Each one of the men chosen would ideally be expected to have skills in at least one or two of the other specialities involved in the venture and to have a working knowledge of English and French. (Icelandic would be a bonus!)

Our aims were explained to each candidate and in particular we made sure that each member was fully aware of the 'ethics' of our proposal to combine the functions of filming and exploring within the same group of men, rather than, as is often the case, having a team of explorers and another team of film-makers. We sought and obtained their assent to this design as it was essential to eradicate misunderstandings at the very outset. With the exception of one member, Jean Jacques Mrejen, each person who finally joined the team was either recommended to us by a friend or was already known to us.

Paul Vander-Molen—kayakist

Mick Coyne—kayakist

Benoit Dabout—kayakist

Gerry Breen—pilot

Bruno Cusa—film cameraman

Jean Jaques Mrejen—sound recorder/
cameraman.

Gudbrandur Jóhansson—driver

Gísli Hjálmarsson—Snowcat driver

Robert Grégoire— photographer

Kári Gudbjörnsson—aircraft support

Simon Baker—pilot

Jeb Stuart—rafter

Jean-Luc Cheron—photographer/doctor

When, after many interviews, training sessions, revisions, selections and rejections, our team for July 1983 had been finalised, it was as follows:

Paul Vander-Molen	(GB)	Kayakist	Expedition Leader
Mick Coyne	(GB)	Kayakist	Co-organiser
Benoit Dabout	(FR)	Kayakist	Co-organiser (France)
John (Jeb) Stuart	(USA)	Rafter	
Gerry Breen	(GB)	Microlight Pilot	Aeronautical Leader
Jean-Luc Cheron	(FR)	Doctor/Photographer	
Robert Grégoire	(FR)	Photographer	
Bruno Cusa	(FR)	Cameraman	
Jean Jacques Mrejen	(FR)	Sound Engineer	
Gísli Hjálmarsson	(IC)	Snowcat/Guide	
Gudbrandur Jóhansson	(IC)	Driver/security	

With the back up team comprising:

Simon Baker	(GB)	2nd Microlight
Didier Lafond	(FR)	2nd Camera (he was later unable to join us).
Bruno Bazin	(FR)	Boat skipper (2nd)*
Marc Bizien	(FR)	Boat skipper (1st)*
Kári Gudbjörnsson	(IC)	Light aircraft

(*The boat skippers came into the team picture purely because of our decision that it would be very worthwhile to travel to Iceland by sail, and apart from the sea crossing, took no further part in the expedition.)

Paul Vander-Molen, 26, British. Expedition Leader. Research Engineer, Fellow of the Royal Geographical Society (also Advisor). Leader of 'Valley of Ice Expedition', 1981. Thirteen years canoeing experience. Also skier and hang-glider. Fluent in French.

Mick Coyne, 25, British. Co-organiser. Studying for B.Sc. Geography and Ecology. Leader of canoeing expeditions to Norway and Austria. Ex-Royal Marine. Thirteen years canoeing experience. Also skier, climber and parachutist.

Benoit Dabout, 20, French. Co-organiser. Studying Civil Engineering. Competed in last five French National Canoeing Championships. Nine years canoeing experience.

Gerry Breen, 30, British. Aeronautical Activities. Chairman of Breen Aviation. World Record holder for motorised hang-glider longest flight; also unofficial altitude record. R.A.F. trained. First microlight flight London to Paris. Also skier.

Jean-Luc Cheron, 25, French. Photographer/Doctor. Physician. First prize Around the World Film Competition, 1978. Worldwide photo distribution following expeditions to Sweden and Alaska (Valley of Ice). Also skier and climber. Fluent in English.

Bruno Cusa, 27, French. Film Cameraman. Leading cameraman reporter for French network Antenne 2. Films include prize-winning 'Valley of Ice' from the expedition on the Alsek in Alaska. Trainee helicopter pilot. Also skier and climber. Fluent in English.

Jean Jacques Mrejen. 23, French. Sound Recordist/Cameraman. Skier, sailor. Speaks Arabic, Italian, Spanish, English.

Gísli Hjálmarsson, 36, Icelandic. Guide, Snowcat Driver, Mechanic. Twenty years experience with all forms of transport, extensive knowledge of glacier. Member of Icelandic Life Saving Association. Speaks English.

Gudbrandur Jóhannson, 33, Icelandic. Driver, Radio, Security. Teacher maths/ physics, First Aider, Ambulance Driver, Member of Icelandic Life Saving Association, skier, climber, hunter, Leader of Sea/Land Rescue Team, Communications expert. Speaks fluent English, Danish.

Robert Grégoire, 41, French. Photographer. Experienced in publicity photography, political and economic sciences. Skier. Speaks French, Spanish, Italian and English.

Kári Gudbjörnsson, 26, Icelandic. Aircraft Support. Air traffic control officer. Hang-glider pilot. Light aircraft licence. Also skier and climber. Fluent English.

Simon Baker, 29, Australian, but living in England. Microlight Instructor. Diploma in Civil Engineering.

John (Jeb) Stuart, 31, American. Rafter, kayakist. Seventeen years experience rafting, kayaking. Professional carpenter, builder.

Reconnaissance II

My second visit to Iceland took place around Easter 1983 and this time I took with me our microlight pilot, Gerry Breen. Part of the reason for this visit was to look for sponsors and also to generally try to open up the opportunities for our expedition. But of equal importance was our decision to reconnoitre the Vatnajökull glacier. Through Kári Gudbjörnsson, whom I had met on my first visit, we were introduced to two Icelandic men who were to become important members of our team, Gísli Hjálmarsson, a glacier guide and Snowcat driver, and Gudbrandur Jóhansson, a driver, radio operator, and a member of the Icelandic Life Saving Association. We were invited to a meal (of reindeer meat, for he is a hunter) at Gísli's home, and we then decided to do some reconnaissance and take some skiddoos on to the glacier.

A skiddoo is a small snow scooter, with an engine rather like the microlight, usually 2-stroke, and skis instead of wheels. Most of them have a single steering bar and a tank-like track at the rear. We thought that with three or four of these and with trailers we could test out how far we could get in four or five hours and at the same time find out about the hazards of the snow cap. We planned to begin our expedition from a town on the south coast called Höfn (pronounced Huppen), and it was from here that we set from Gísli's house, to make our first encounter with the great glacier—Vatnajökull.

The sun shone, the ice sparkled, the air was crisp, and we were making headway. It was exhilarating, and we decided to have some fun. Gerry, able to ski, but not the most expert among us, decided to put on skis and to attach a rope and cross bar to the back of a skidoo, to be towed over the ice like a water skier behind a motor boat. It looked marvellous, so we all had a go. The ground was bumpy, with undulating slopes and with crusty snow. The skiddoos got faster. And faster. They can travel at a surprising 30 to 45 mph on suitable snow. Suddenly Gerry struck a bump at speed. He shot into the air for several yards and came down heavily on another bump. He was shaken, but in typical manner, shrugged it off. Later we discovered he had broken a rib, and he was not too pleased about that. We skylarked some more with the skiddoos, driving them at speed up a steep, almost vertical slope. The Icelanders were very expert at this, knowing just when to apply brake and when to turn. When I tried, I parted company with the machine at the very top of the incline. Fortunately neither the machine nor I was hurt, and it says much for the toughness of the skiddoo that it can survive very rough handling. (In actual fact, the weather being kind, we travelled further in a total of eight

hours, including our return, than we were able to move during the entire Iceland Breakthrough episode on the Vatnajökull glacier.)

This trip on the glacier showed me the resilience of Gerry. In pain, he kept his sense of humour, cracking jokes the whole time, and although cold and tired, on the journey back to Höfn he gave me a lesson in meteorology and navigation. An excellent teacher, he showed me how to recognise weather fronts and to assess probabilities of approaching winds and storms. I was completely sure that in asking Gerry to join our venture as our principal pilot we had made a superb choice.

When we finally got back to town, we met up with Kári Gudbjörnsson, and learned that his friend Ivar, the engraver, whom we had met on our first trip to Iceland, had a plane. He agreed to pilot us down the course of the Jökulsá River. We started towards Höfn and then flew across the glacier towards Kverkfjöll where, with a feeling of great satisfaction I was able to identify two V-shaped mountains with a glacier between them, looking from the air exactly as I had seen them in a three dimensional map with Mick back in London.

From our considerable height the river below us looked very small, meandering, like a black snake, occasionally splitting and braiding and every now and then completely disappearing. The surrounding scenery was all white and we thought the disappearance of the river might be due to some broader shallow reaches being frozen over and having then been covered in with a sprinkling of snow. I took a video film from the plane and gained great respect for the task confronting our cameramen—in no time at all I had a headache and was quite unable to hold the thing still long enough to get a picture. However, my amateur film was to prove a very useful tool when we got back to England.

Onwards we flew, sighting the waterfall Selfoss, the first of four mighty falls. Selfoss is horseshoe shaped, looking for all the world as though a giant had placed his heel in the river. From our altitude the water looked fairly quiet between falls. (From the flow rate charts we had studied we would expect this—the volume of water increases as summer progresses.) We passed over the powerful Dettifoss, greatest of them all, ringed with spray and difficult to read. It appeared to be partly frozen over. Because of a peculiarity in the angle at which the fall is set into the canyon, air turbulence is severe and would present considerable danger to our fliers. As we flew along the canyon, filming with our video, we thought we saw rapids—more useful information. We judged this part of our trip to have been highly rewarding.

Our quest for sponsors was equally successful. We met on this visit, Thor Asgeisson, the Managing Director of Olís Oils, whose enthusiasm resulted in his company becoming a very major sponsor, supplying us with fuel, vehicles and facilities. We also met people from the Höfn Co-op (K.A.S.K) who generously offered us free food and provisions. A company named Alafoss, who made beautiful Icelandic Wool Sweaters entered into a sponsorship arrangement with us in return for publicity, as did also a firm named 66° North, who promised us special rainwear and underclothing.

When Gerry and I arrived back and reported all this to Mick, the three of us agreed that our second reconnaissance trip had been remarkably successful, in every way. After discussing all our technical findings we told Mick about some of the lighter moments—including the story of just one of the many incidents of Icelandic hospitality.

We had been invited to 'The Family House' by our hosts, the delightful and welcoming Erlingur and Andrea. We were shown into a beautiful room, where a large,

Left: **The view from the Jökulsárlón lake looking up at part of the 70-mile stretch of ice that is the Vatnajökull glacier.**

heavily carved table was set for family and some guests. Each place had elegant cutlery and a decorative table mat, besides which was a glass of Schnapps. With due decorum we were asked to be seated and were told that we should take part in a little Icelandic ceremony.

The door opened and a platter was brought in—we were each of us served with three or four small cubes of flesh, which our hosts proceeded to eat with obvious relish. Gerry and I detected a strange aroma—somewhat acrid and ammoniac. We looked at each other—we sniffed again—yes, it was a strong smell of ammonia, and it seemed to come from our plates! The rules of hospitality imply that the guest plays his part in the scenario, and it was therefore incumbent upon us to *eat* and *enjoy* this ceremonial offering. The spirit was willing but *our* flesh was weak. I took one mouthful and leapt from the table to retreat in haste to the kitchen. Gerry was quite unable to bring himself to actually put the cube in his mouth. We tried again, for we had to uphold British tradition—but no way.

'What is it?' we enquired.

'Don't you like it? It is an Icelandic delicacy—it's shark meat—*raw* shark meat'.

We wondered at the acrid taste, but when they informed us that it is first hung for six months and then buried in the ground for a further six months, we understood only too well and wondered where in fact it had been buried! Our hosts, gentle as always, put us completely at our ease and after a memorable and delicious meal we retired contentedly to bed.

Training and the Team

As time elapsed, our team began to grow, and we each trained hard at our particular skills in our various countries, myself with the help of Mick organising the British section, Benoit Dabout organising the French, leaving the Icelanders to organise themselves.

We were an assorted bunch, some tall, some short, some heavy, some light, bearded, clean shaven, dark, fair and from widely different backgrounds. The details requested in personal dossiers were extensive even to the point of asking for inside leg measurements and particular food preferences. My own reply to this last question was 'Lots of steak and dumplings'. For some reason that eludes me, no one gave me any of this during the whole of the expedition!

Although each of us had certain skills for which, in the main, we were chosen to take part in Iceland Breakthrough, there were some skills common to most of the team which gave us additional strength in the testing conditions we were to encounter. Almost every member of the team could ski, some expertly, some adequately. Several of us could handle a kayak; once again, some in violent water, some on the quieter reaches. We could all drive; we all had learned to deal with the cold. Many of us were bi- or multi-lingual, although only the Icelanders spoke Icelandic, a fascinating language which sounds akin to Welsh, with emphasis on double 'L' and a lyrical approach to description.

For many months we met as frequently as we could, for training sessions in river techniques, flying performances, survival exercises and the many other lessons we had to imbibe before the journey could be undertaken with some sense of preparedness. We learned about each other, we tested the interface between our skills and our personalities, one person with another and slowly from the tributaries of ideas and aspirations came the smoother flow of a trained team working towards a common goal—the conquest of Jökulsá. And the excitement grew.

Because of the international nature of our venture, training tended to polarise to three centres (England, France and Iceland), and it involved quite a lot of liaison work travelling about. We never managed to get the whole team together at one time before Iceland. On a large number of occasions groups within the team stayed at our house, in North London, much to the amusement (or bemusement) of my mother. I should explain perhaps that she is a super cook and knowing that a horde of hungry Frenchmen were about to descend upon her, got quite worried about putting on Cordon Bleu dishes. Imagine her amazement when it transpired that what these gourmets really wanted was mostly baked beans with lashings of tomato sauce! She has not completely recovered from this shock, but my father, who has a grand appetite, is trying to get her back on course.

As regards the actual training, careful thought had to be given to our aims and objectives. Our training should encompass a number of things. Of course, first and foremost would be the practising and polishing of our individual skills as far as we were able. Then would be the acclimatisation to the cold. Each person had his own methods; some sought out the coldest water, others lived in unheated rooms, other took cold showers—and in our own ways we gradually hardened our bodies for the conditions we expected. As it turned out, they were on some occasions rather worse than we had thought, and very testing.

While training we worked out our communication systems and allocated areas of responsibility to each member. We also had discussion sessions when problems were highlighted, and everyone present could contribute their ideas for solving them. Slowly, slowly a shape emerged. Slowly, slowly, each man began to gain confidence in his role. We found each other's strengths and weaknesses. We adapted to each other, in varying degrees. We learned of national temperaments and of the difficulties of language.

The natural grouping of the expedition in three countries caused certain problems, but these were in the main overcome by the expertise of our highly experienced team and by frequent liaison visits. For this reason, I did not confine myself to training within any particular group, and instead I floated between the groups, visiting the countries concerned, as necessary.

In England our contingent comprised myself, Mick Coyne, Gerry Breen and Simon Baker, our second microlight pilot. In France Benoit Dabout liaised with Jean Luc Cheron, Bruno Cusa, Jean Jacques Mrejen, and Robert Grégoire, as team members. He also had connections with the two skippers of the sailing boat which was to take us to Iceland. And in Iceland, the team consisted of Gísli Hjálmarsson, Gudbrandur Jóhansson, and Kári Gudbjörnsson.

We have already learned of the accomplishments of Mick Coyne, and it is appropriate now to enlarge upon other members of the British-based section of our team: Gerry Breen and Simon Baker.

Firstly then, about Gerry, our first microlight pilot, it is universally agreed that he is one of the outstanding fliers of our time. During his career as a flier he has notched up many records and while running the largest Microlight School in Europe, was also engaged in selling Hybrid Micros for an American company. He has run a hang-gliding school in Wales. A brilliant flier, he is also an expert practical mechanic and well founded in the maintenance of the machines he flies. He has some 3000 flying hours to his credit in a great variety of machines, and, as his personality demands, uses all his skills to the ultimate in flying. RAF trained, he is an expert in survival and has a particular flair for navigation and meteorology. Supremely optimistic and with a ready wit, he is a valued friend, and as a member of the team, a hardworking innovator. His experience in film making for a cigarette company and in stunt flying for feature films were invaluable on the expedition.

Medium of height, with brown curly hair and a light beard, he dresses with casual elegance and this, with his infectious smile, and excitement of manner make him a charismatic personality. He at present runs a Microlight School in Portugal—he adores the sunshine!

Although Simon Baker was only in Iceland for the second half of the expedition, he was indeed a valuable member. He was chosen for his immense ability that had been proven many times whilst working alongside Gerry Breen at Gerry's flying school. His job on the expedition was to fly the kayakists and Jeb over difficult stretches of rapids so they could get some idea of the problems ahead and the best way to tackle them, and to carry members of the technical team for filming and photography. The pilots' contribution to the success of the film and photographs shouldn't be underestimated for it was they who had to get the photographers into those incredible positions and remain calm even when committing themselves to dangerous situations. When flying with Bruno in particular, the microlight had to be kept moving very smoothly—so in itself the film is testimony to the pilots' expertise.

As a team member, Simon was always willing to help out and made a valuable contribution in both manpower and ideas. Not only is Simon a good pilot, but he is also a good teacher and he passed on many of his skills to the rest of us. A quiet and unassuming character, his amiability and reliability made him popular both within the team and amongst the Icelandic people we came into contact with.

The French section was co-ordinated by Benoit Dabout. Benoit was the 'Benjamin' of our twelve tribesmen. At twenty, he was the junior by at least about five years, but in his short life he had climbed to great heights of athletic prowess and in particular had become a superb kayakist of National Competition class. A strong, steady young man, well built, with brown hair, he is the middle son of five brothers and a sister, all of whom are kayak enthusiasts. The canoe club to which I belonged in France was situated near his home at Joinville le Pont on the river Marne and during the three or four years in which Benoit and I had been friends, I had trained there with him many times.

As a person, Benoit was quiet, but with firm convictions. Like most men of twenty he had a voracious appetite and needed large amounts of sleep. During the expedition the catch phrase 'Where's Benoit?' was indicative of his occasional absence buried deep in a sleeping bag, but he was always good humoured about being brought back to the busy world and would set to with a will. Professionally he was training as a Civil Engineer, specialising in Quantity Surveying (which could be a useful skill for anyone contemplating acting as Quartermaster to an expedition). However, in the context of

Iceland Breakthrough, his function apart from being one of the main kayakists, was to be the French Co-ordinator and organiser, a task which he performed very well in the light of his relative inexperience. He had no conflicts with anyone and was a valued member of the expedition, making a considerable contribution to our waterborne exploits. In the river he had the sureness of touch that is the hallmark of the great kayakist, and above all, he was an impeccable judge not only of the water but of his own abilities and limits. He was a very safe, but very versatile white water traveller. His command of English improved as the expedition moved on.

It is not easy to recall how we met with all the members of the team. Two other members were known to me from our 'Valley of Ice' adventure of 1981 and had at that time proved themselves to be exceptional men in so many ways—men with whom I had already established lasting friendships and for whom I had the highest esteem. These were Jean-Luc Cheron and Bruno Cusa.

Jean-Luc combined the qualifications of Doctor of Medicine, with consummate skills as a photographer. A lively, highly gifted man, he has a penchant for adventure, as extracts from his personal dossier show. Under 'Training and Experience' he had answered 'Physician, 9 years study, Cardiac (1 year) Surgery (6 months). Thesis—film in preparation. Photographer: Prize—best film in a French TV broadcast (Antenne 2) *La Course Autour du Monde* in 1978. Member of expedition 'Valley of Ice' Alaska, and Yukon 1981; 700 miles by camel in Sahara 1979'—and so on. We were delighted to have Jean-Luc on our team as our doctor, photographer and nutritional expert.

Bruno Cusa was our cameraman. My memory takes me back to France, a few years earlier, when a team from our canoe club in Paris, having 'obtained' tyres and other items with which to build a raft, proceeded to a river in the south, and after a great deal of experimentation, launched it on white water. The water rapidly became very turbulent until the craft, out of control, turned over. Those aboard were thrown into the water. Bruno as well. He checked to see if the others were safe and finding they were not in need of his help, swam to a nearby rock, got out a Leica and with supreme calm proceeded to take a series of so-called 'still' photographs of this turbulent scene. I thought then as I think now, that any man with that sort of 'cool,' any man with that sort of dedication had to be a very special man. Bruno Cusa is a very special man, with quiet strength, superb knowledge of his craft of filming, and wide-ranging physical skills, not least of which is the ability to fly a helicopter. He encounters danger with no fuss, plays his team role perfectly, but with it all retains his highly individual style. The beautiful films taken of 'Valley of Ice' and later 'Iceland Breakthrough' are testimony to the 'state of the art' as practised by Cusa the film maker. Bruno was available for 'Iceland Breakthrough' and he was asked to join. We now had our cameraman—the best!

Robert Grégoire, at forty-one the oldest of the team, a slender, fit-looking man, was a professional photographer and his role was to take still pictures of all aspects of the expedition, while Jean Jacques Mrejen, who came as a newly qualified cameraman, with knowledge and some experience of sound recording, almost as a reserve, proved his worth as a superb sound recordist, and at times doubled up for Bruno Cusa during the expedition.

John 'Jeb' Stuart, was the only American on the team and was quite unknown to us, although he came highly recommended. Aged thirty-one, he has travelled all over the

U.S.A. as an itinerant carpenter, working on power stations, in coal mines, on bridges and in condominiums. Hailing originally from Aurora, Colorado, he is a highly respected rafter with at least seventeen years' experience, and a very good kayakist as well. He is single, and lives in San Diego. Jeb is a very large, powerful man, 6′ 2″ tall, weighing almost 14 stone. A tower of a man, he became a tower of strength to us and a very popular member of Iceland Breakthrough.

The Icelandic members of the team were, of course, very much at home and in fact possessed knowledge and skills which were essential to the expedition. Each was a strong and interesting personality, with typical Icelander's pride in his country. Gudbrandur Jóhansson, short, stockily built, became a very popular member of the expedition, fulfilling his main function as radio communications expert cum transport manager and driver extraordinaire. His enthusiasm for this mode of travel occasionally led him to some excesses on the road, but, this apart, he was completely reliable and without fail, delivered his promises on time.

We had stayed with him and his wife in their pleasant bungalow at Höfn, where she, an excellent cook, had sometimes regaled us with such dishes as succulent lamb cooked in a piquant white sauce. He had an excellent command of English (despite his occasional reluctance to translate Icelandic comments!) and his general enthusiasm for our venture, his knowledge of the terrain, and his popularity among his peers, not only ensured his successful participation in our journey, but enabled him to introduce us to some sponsors, with great advantage to our plans.

Gísli, our glacier guide and Snowcat driver, was about 5′ 9″ tall, heavily built and heavily bearded with strong features and a handsome appearance. Gísli gave a first impression of having lived a hard life, a true impression for he had always worked extremely long hours, using his consummate skills as a welder and a coach builder to great effect. He had absolute command of many manual skills, as evidenced by the excellent cabin he built for our Snowcat, almost single handed, during the spring of our year. Strong as an ox, his personality matched his physique. Proud, as are Icelanders, he showed on occasions the brooding temperament known in the tales called Sagas—an inheritance from the Vikings—of which band of men, he could well have been a descendant. He was proud too of his wife Soffie and their baby, and of their beautiful home, of polished wood and airy spotless rooms, and of the unstinting hospitality it enabled them to provide. In whatever occasional clashes of temperament arose between Gísli and other members of the team, there was always deep down, the healthy respect that men of action engender between them, and the friendships which were welded together during our days on the glacier have remained close and true.

Our third Icelander, Kári, a pilot, was to act in reserve with light aircraft, and gave us very valuable assistance on a number of occasions. Not least, he was instrumental in making very many valuable contacts for us.

Although our three team sections were beginning to work as a whole, it became apparent that not only was there the polarisation of nationality, but there was a certain natural grouping concerned with inherent skills. Thus, with the exception of Benoit Dabout, who of course was the co-ordinator and a superb kayakist, the remainder of the French contingent were completely identified with the filming, photographing and recording of the expedition. In this, Jean-Luc played a dual role as the expedition's doctor/photographer. There was also some natural grouping of the Icelanders, because of their knowledge of the terrain. However, to the great credit of every member of this international team, these tendencies were never allowed to become barriers to the general goodwill and to the progress of the expedition.

My role of liaison increased in intensity as the time wore on towards our starting date, but gradually it all seemed to be coming together, and our enthusiasm grew with every passing day. The kayakists took every possible opportunity to keep in training, and practised rescue procedures and special techniques for the water we expected to encounter. Where possible we took microlight flights and were given lessons in handing these wonderfully manoeuvrable craft. The photographers looked to their equipment and Jean-Luc addressed himself to the problems of nutrition and medicine in cold climates, while Mick, our climbing leader, set about organising his specialised gear.

The training went on and we became more of a team. One day we would get to Iceland.

Leadership

Given a team of twelve specialists, each known for his positive approach to the job in hand, it would be impossible to have an overall leader of the 'Command' school. The word 'leader' in this context then rather becomes 'organiser' and there is a fine distinction.

The role of this 'leader/organiser' is subtle—he must at most times be the motivator, the prime mover and where required the spur or the brake. But at other times, when the central role to be played in a situation is necessarily the province of one of the specialists, he must temporarily relinquish control and allow the specialist to make decisions, not only on his own behalf but for all the team in so far as they may be affected by what is planned. It was obvious, for example, that when a situation demanded that Gerry flew over the lake, he would be unquestionably in charge of all flying procedures, and would make all the necessary decisions. My role at this time would be one of (a) definition of Gerry's intentions, (b) agreement of the feasibility of the project, and (c) the dovetailing in of other team members in whatever activity was demanded. The leader/organiser thereby became more of an organiser for the time being but retaining still his objective of motivation. The subtleties of this are shown by the various changes in the command situation. As a further example, at a time when I might have considered it was too dangerous for raft or kayak to run a section of rapid, I would have made a command decision to hold which would be accepted by all the team, whereas in certain other sections in which cross winds would preclude the use of rafts, but would allow kayaks, I would pass the role of leader to Jeb as 'officer in charge of rafting' and by implication 'other water activities' and Jeb would make any decision to delay until winds had dropped. I would then take over the role of leader/organiser again and manage to get the team 'slotted' into the scenario.

But more than this, the leader must understand the potential for chafing at the interfaces of national characters. He must be aware of tensions, challenges, strains and fissures in the whole make-up of the team, and he must anticipate and dissipate negative tendencies. Such a role is taxing. But the rewards are great and the lessons worth the learning.

The Ground Rules

The approach to organising an expedition passes through a number of stages. There is first of all the initial excitement and the early heady days of assessing the practicalities of turning an idea into reality. Following on from this the work diverges from its central theme into a number of tasks, such as choice of personnel, fund raising, equipment and so on. It is just at this time, *before* the organiser goes too far on any of these lines, that there needs to be a disciplined approach to the rules which will govern the proposed venture. One or two of the main aims will of course have been set out, and general agreement to them would be necessary among the early nucleus of the explorers before any progress would be made, but more than these aims, it would be necessary to state and obtain assent to the principles and ethics envisaged. It may not always be clear to the outside world just what the expedition sets out to achieve, by what means and within what parameters, and the facts must be stated clearly and publicly as soon as there is clear intent to proceed.

To give an example of 'the rules of the game,' as it were, let us look at the most complex expedition ever mounted. This of course was the astounding feat of landing Neil Armstrong on the moon. It may seem obvious to state but the absolute rule in the planning, design and execution of this wonderful exploit was *not* just to get a man *to* the moon, but to get a man *back* from the moon. This rule would have permeated every aspect of the work. No single piece of calculation, drawing, or prototype would have been processed through without this rule being the over-riding background consideration. Then there are ethics or rules on a more personal level. A man setting out to perform a special feat will make a statement in which he imposes certain limits. Thus Ranulf Fiennes made a commitment to circumnavigate the globe. Among his 'ground rules' he stated (a) that he would pass through both the North and South Pole and (b) he would only travel on the surface and at no time would he use air travel as a means to achieve his goal. These are arbitrary rules, but they impose a certain ethic and discipline on the expedition members and serve not only to ensure a tight and tidy approach to the job in hand, but an understanding and acceptance on the part of the general public, among whom there may well be many sponsors. They, in particular, have entitlement to know what will be the firm framework of the endeavour.

For our expedition, we set out our aims very early in the scheme of things and in the main these were adhered to. Certain modifications were enforced upon us by unforeseen calamities in the course of the expedition, but at no time did we transgress the rules which we had laid down pursuant to these aims. Before stating these rules, it may help to point up the principles involved if we realise that there may be certain conflicts in the matter of 'film-making' and 'pure exploration' on the first part, and on the second, there may be conflict between the 'purist sportsman' and the 'entrepreneurial innovator'.

To take the first part. There is a natural divide between the team approach to an expedition and the film-making approach to it. It would, in most circumstances, result in having on the one side a team of experts performing their skills and getting on with the project under their leader(s), and on the other hand, running somewhat in parallel with them, a film-making crew, under *its* director. The expedition would thus have two leaders, and conflict would be almost inevitable, particularly when the interests of film making would make demands that the 'pure' explorer would find unacceptable—such as, having to go back and re-negotiate a difficult passage, in order to get a better film because, for example, the light changed or the camera angles needed improving. There would also be the problem that the film director would want to have considerable say *before* any particular aspect was put into action, so that his team could get themselves into position for filming. And so on. The potential for disagreement is large. This however, is not to say that harmony cannot be achieved—history has proved that it can be made to work, but disciplines are necessary to ensure *proper* working.

The rules as far as this particular side of the project was concerned, were that we would in fact do our own filming and recording as we went along. That we would in fact be a combination team of explorers and film makers under one main form of leadership. For this reason and quite central to the whole operation, it was essential to have a team with expertise in both spheres. We were very fortunate to include such men in the group. We needed to state at the outset that we would be making a film as we explored, and that the implications of this must be understood and accepted by every team member. Implied in this discipline would be the confidence that the 'Director/Leader/Organiser' and his cohorts could perform the task and deliver the goods. But then, no one will go on an expedition if he thinks the organiser cannot do the job! So much for the subtle differences between exploring and filming, and how in our case, we made the rule to combine them in the same men.

We then proceed to the public statement of our technique. There are those 'purist' kayakists who find the combination of a kayak and a microlight not quite acceptable, and we can honour their view. However, in the instance of opening up a new method of exploration, we made a public clarification of our intent, and sought full acceptance of this from all potential team members before they could be included in the final selection. It might be a fact, although we didn't find it so, that the 'purist' microlight pilot would be ill at ease with the idea of using his plane in the way in which we envisaged, and it was necessary for this purpose to ensure that all members knew and understood the ethics of our intention.

To sum up—the organisers of an expedition must be clear in their own minds about their aims and objectives, and then, quite early in the preparations, they must make public and clear, exactly what are the means they intend to employ, laying down demarcation lines for the guidance of team members, and for the information of the sponsors and the public at large. And in practice, they must abide by these rules.

Timing and Logistics

The complexities of making sure that each person would arrive at the right place with the proper gear and in time to mesh in with others, kept our minds lively and exercised. We had to engage a boat and its crew, and ensure that they were ready and equipped for departure day. All members of the team except the Icelanders and Jeb were to assemble at my house several days before departure date for packing and final preparation. This all needed to be organised, as did also the obtaining of passports, visas, customs forms, and many other things. We had to arrange a special wave band on the boat's radio. We had to ensure that we had the right amount of transport to get the equipment on to the boat and that those of us who were to travel with her had all the right gear, to say nothing of the means of getting to the boat from Hendon. We had to organise a Press Day in Iceland, and to get the team and its gear from Höfn, our landing port, to Reykjavík, where Press Day was arranged. Lists were made, and lists were ticked. Lists were added to, and then the additions were ticked, and gradually the organisation began to work and our plan to look good.

The plan to travel to Iceland by sail was not without its difficulties. We had been put in touch with the builders of three 50-foot (16 m) ketches with retractable keels, which were intended for use in an expedition to the South Pole in 1985. It was agreed that we were to test one of these, *Basile,* together with a crew of two, in time for the builders to make final refinements for the Polar work. Five weeks before Iceland Breakthrough was to commence, we received a call from the owner to say that *Basile* would not be ready in time. What were we to do? Time was now so short. *Basile* would have been ideal—we could have put all our team and equipment on board—and now we had to start looking again. We were unable to get a boat from any of our sponsors, and so we scoured magazines, advertisements, explored boat yards, and as a priority, alerted all team members to hunt for a suitable vessel. I was determined, and so were the others, to find a way to arrive by sail.

Then we heard that there was a boat for charter, berthed in the Isle of Skye at Sleat Marine. Mick checked her out and came back to say that *Goodbye Girl* would do for our journey, but that she was too small for our equipment. It was therefore decided that Mick and Robert would go to Reykjavík by ferry from Newcastle, with most of the heavy equipment, while Bruno, Jean-Luc, Jean Jacques, Benoit, myself and the two 'skippers' (both friends of Benoit), would take the boat from Skye to Höfn. It was now just two weeks away from our departure date—so much to do—so little time in which to do it!

I first saw *Goodbye Girl* when we arrived at Mallaig to embark and my reaction was a dismayed 'Bloody hell! How can we all get in that little boat?' *Goodbye Girl* was a 34-foot (10m) sloop of Bermudian Rig—that is a triangular jib or fore-sail and a large triangular mainsail. She was sleek, white, and looked fast. We had a beautiful red and blue spinnaker which we could hoist for running before the wind, and she handled well on all points of sailing; she had a reserve engine and a 30-gallon (135-litre) tank. But she did not have a retractable keel and we had to abandon one of our original ideas, which was to haul her up onto the same stretch of shore on which the first settlers had arrived in Iceland over a thousand years ago.

To illustrate the complexities of planning, we had to conform to a special safety system instituted by Hannes Hafstein. It was called Duty Reporting System. Charts of a wide area surrounding Iceland, and embracing the British Isles, were drawn into boxes, each with a number. From our radio in *Goodbye Girl* we were obliged to report twice daily at a prearranged fixed time, say between 10.00 – 13.30 and 20.00 – 22.00 hours. On leaving Skye we were to open up on Channel 16 frequency and contact Stornoway, who would then instruct us to change to a notified frequency. We were to report our 'Box' position by its number. The principle of the system is that failure to report on two successive occasions at the prearranged time will automatically alert the life saving organisations that something is amiss. On the planning side, nothing could be left to chance. We had to ensure that the correct radio was aboard and that the operators understood the box system. International radio communication is in English, and we had to make sure that this could be complied with.

There was to be a replacement crew from Paris, for the return of the boat (and by a miracle of timing they arrived at Höfn on the same day as we arrived!) They would expect to find the boat ready in every respect and were to take it around the coast for four or five days to get used to it, before returning it to Scotland. Food had to be arranged for them and many other things besides, and our planning lists became longer and longer, and more and more complicated. But we kept on ticking them inexorably as the time became shorter and shorter.

At this point it might be appropriate to pay tribute to the Life Saving Association of Iceland, of which both Gísli and Gudbrandur were members. Their brochure explains briefly how they are organised, their plans for the future, and their justifiable pride in their history. What it does not tell the reader is of the dedication and courage of the volunteers who have made it their responsibility to go to the aid of those in distress. Courage indeed, for when Icelandic weather is bad, it is very bad and only the brave and the strong may challenge it.

Equipment

Events would prove that our initial aims would have to be modified, but at this early stage we had a well thought-out working plan which we set out to organise in practical terms. Our lists of requirements were endless: clothing, skis, special boots, survival clothing, tents, climbing gear, a generator, fuel, heating equipment, rations, transport, skiddoos, a Snowcat, trailers, microlights, kayaks, rafts, paddles, oars, life jackets, medicine, cameras, film, drinks, spades, helmets, goggles, toiletries and much more besides. Each person was to be responsible for that equipment directly related to his own speciality—but in the general matter of stores, organisation was largely undertaken by Mick Coyne and myself.

One of the problems which can arise when attempting to work through sponsors, is that equipment may be delayed until the last minute which, in some cases, could be too late. For example, we had ordered special boots which we understood would require some weeks of wear to break them in. These special boots serve principally as a climbing boot and can be fitted with crampons for ice work. It is also possible to walk around in them (although they are not the perfect walking boot) and they can be used with skis. It was quite essential to make sure that team members had a correct fit and that they had become used to the boots.

As far as was practicable, we tried to ensure that training was performed using the actual or identical equipment to that planned for the expedition. Lives may depend upon split second judgement based on an almost automatic response to the machine in hand, which, by constant practice should become almost an extension of oneself.

Having equipment in England or France was no guarantee that it would work out in the rigours of the Icelandic climate, and so we took every opportunity of testing our goods in difficult situations. The Snowcat of course was Gísli's province. Surprisingly, the skiddoos became the pet of Gudbrandur who was very expert in handling them. Much of our equipment came from sponsors with direct connections in the field of 'outdoor activities'. Obviously, there would be a publicity value for such firms if we were to be seen wearing or using their products. And in some cases, there was an element of testing the goods as well. On the score of clothing, we had four main types. A British firm run by a couple named Bovil, supplied us with SP 27 jackets. Each member of the team had one; they were lightweight and warm and in the course of the expedition came in for a lot of use. There was a problem in certain conditions in that the material used for the outer 'skin' became heavy and retained water when wetted, which froze hard in the lowest of temperatures, turning the jacket into armour plating, and then, when temperatures were raised, still retained the moisture from the melt. Fortunately, it did not penetrate through, but up on the glacier these jackets were very stiff indeed. Apart from this, they were well designed and we were very glad to have them with us. The heavily padded suits we wore for maximum warmth in severe conditions and which doubled up as flying suits, were the Ozee suits. These were made in Britain and were quite superb products. For the cold weather the full length body and leg zips were worn completely closed, but when the weather warmed up, we would undo them which allowed the suits to aerate. They were by far the most popular of all our clothes.

From Damart, based in both England and France, we obtained warm poly-propylene underclothing. We had full length long-johns, long-sleeved vests, gloves and hats. We wore these all the time and even used them under our wet suits. They were without question excellent products in design and manufacture. An Icelandic company, called 66° North, were very enthusiastic about our venture. Their products were an orange-coloured waterproof and a warm fibre pile suit, both of them extremely well made. They also supplied us with special bootee-like socks and woolly-pile hats and fur ones like balaclavas. These were our four main clothing suppliers.

Our skis were made by Duret. They were yellow and suitable for soft conditions and with emery bindings. They were suitable for the conditions we encountered but did not actually come in for very hard use. Our climbing equipment, we bought mostly in France where it was cheaper than England. Some of it was Mick's own property. We used two thicknesses of rope 9 mm and 11 mm both in modern 'kermantle'. When purchased, these ropes are in 980-foot (300-m) lengths and it is usual to cut them to make two. We took four of these with us but retained one full 980-foot (300-m) length one for special use in the canyon by Dettifoss, as Mick, knowing the great depth of the canyon at this spot wanted at least one rope long enough to descend down to the bottom. Harnesses were of several types, among them being a Willans Sit Harness which we purchased, while some of the team had French chest harnesses.

We wore Joe Brown crash hats, which we begged and borrowed from friends. Our ice screws, which were very useful for the cave descent, were of two lengths: 5 inches (12 cms) and 8 inches (20 cms). They were hollow aluminium tubes with a broad self-cutting thread and rings on the top, plus a hammering block. We hammered them into the ice until the thread began to 'bite' and then inserting the pick end of the hammer into a ring, turned the screw until the thread locked down into the ice solidly. We had some metal devices called jumars, which enable a climber to ascend back up a rope and in conjunction with these, we carried étriers which are small sling-type ladders. We also carried an ample supply of slings. We used a variety of safety rings called carabiners, which Mick brought from England. These were made by Clog of North Wales.

For climbing on ice, we used special 12-spike crampons in which two of the spikes were at the toes and could be kicked into the face of an ice cliff when 'front pointing'—that is vertical climbing. We also brought rock climbing equipment, with aluminium blocks for placing into rocks for the attachment of ropes. We used these in setting up the security arrangements at Dettifoss. We also brought various pitons, which are a sort of metal peg to be driven into rocks, but we did not use these on this occasion.

Our tents were supplied by Ultimate, and were called Phazer Dome. I have described them in detail elsewhere in the story. Ultimate also supplied our sleeping bags and although at the outset we had some problems in that we had chosen unwisely, we were able, eventually, to exchange them for warmer ones and found that Ultimate really came up trumps as regards equipment and helpfulness.

Of course, there were many, many other items which we had to obtain, some of which have been mentioned in earlier chapters and some which will be covered more fully in 'Expeditions Cost Money', where sponsorship is discussed. A glance in the appendices at the list which we supplied to HM Customs and Excise will give some idea of the complexity of supplies for a twelve man expedition to an ever changing environment, which called for the exercise of numerous disciplines.

Food, Wonderful Food?

One of the most important items in equipping an expedition is undoubtedly food. In choosing what to take, the considerations were to be those of calorie requirement, weight/bulk storage, ease of transport and personal preferences, the latter being a vital consideration. Our general aim was to provide a basic 5000 calories per day, per man, with a wide variety of foods. In addition, each man could carry supplementary bags of nuts, raisins or dried bananas to eat at will. On a journey such as ours, and particularly in cold climates, it is advisable to eat rather more than less, but we had to try to restrict foodstuffs to be suitable to each particular stage of the venture. For instance, the storage of foods for transporting on the rafts, had to be approached quite differently from rations carried in flight, and while each kayakist carried in his boat emergency food for two days, this would have to be those items which could be tightly packed into a plastic bag and stowed in a canoe.

We had tea chests, which contained rations sufficient for 12–14 men (the full team) for three days. We also had stout blue plastic barrels which we obtained from Höfn where they were used for fish loading. These would contain a full team's food sufficient for four days. In these the goods were first stowed in plastic bags and these were then put into a stout black plastic bag, to reduce the smell of fish (not always successfully!). The advantage of these barrels was that they could be sealed, and were thus very useful on rafts and on the glacier when conditions were hard. As time progressed, the tea-chests became less used and we ended up with only the barrels.

Jean-Luc Cheron, our doctor/photographer was in charge of the provisions. He did an admirable job in allocation of calories, but was unfortunate in receiving from a sponsor, a considerable quantity of dehydrated food which proved to be quite inedible. We learned the very important lesson for all explorers—before the expedition, every member should sample *and cook* all items of the food provided. There was, as one might have expected, rather an emphasis on French food since almost half of our number were French and the organiser of the food had a predilection for 'Canard à l'Orange'! But these were minor hiccups.

We had made an arrangement whereby at certain strategic points along our intended route, where there were farms or places of storage, we would have a supply of fresh food available, but our general intention was to have overall enough food for the full team for seven or eight weeks. We had radio contact with K.A.S.K., the Co-op in Höfn who helped to organise the pick-up areas.

I have made the point about weight/bulk factors in the carrying of food and at no time was this more important than when Gerry and I took a microlight over the glacier. The following list illustrates the considerable amount of food which has to be carried in reserve, even for a short journey. Stored in a flexible plastic container, with sealable roll-over tops which clipped down, approximately 18 foot x 6 inches x 3 inches, and tied in under the microlight seat, were the following goods: tea bags, sugar, coffee, dehydrated soup satchets, hard rations for each man for one day (in tin boxes with 2-year shelf life) two tins of Delpeyrat (in this case 'Cassoulet au Confit de Canard' was one and the other was 'Salade au Poulet et aux Oeufs de Caille! if my memory is correct). These were rather elaborate mixed French dishes in sealed tins which could be opened without a tin opener. The tins can be used for cooking. Then we had bars of chocolate, dried Swedish biscuits, cheese, bags of nuts, raisins and dried bananas and a bag of mixed spices. All of this, plus some survival equipment weighed very little, but we took it all just for a one hour trip across a glacier. It would have to suffice for three or four days in the event of a crash.

One very nice piece of equipment we had was a portable cooker. This was a cylinder 6 inches in diameter and about 3" high, designed in Sweden, which Bruno Cusa had brought with him. It had several nesting containers within it and when they were removed, a burner was exposed on which a windshield fitted, which in turn, would allow one of the food containers to rest on it for cooking. The heat source was petrol, fed from another cylinder which clipped on to the side of the burner and the starting flame was primed by petrol jelly. The heat of a vaporised petrol flame is intense and this tiny gadget was an extremely efficient cooker. We also took water in army type flasks and as a back-up for heat, some firelighters.

Choice has to be made in all such cases. For this one-hour trip the choice was between taking a tent in case of an accident or taking a fold-up spade with plastic bags, so as to dig an ice cave for shelter. We plumped for the spade and bags. As it happened, when we needed help, it was not on the ice and the spade was not much use—in the same circumstances we would have made the same choice again—such is the nature of providence.

(A full list of food that we took on the expedition can be found in the appendices.)

Microlights and Kayaks

In the UK the definition of a microlight aircraft is an aircraft of less than 330 pounds (150 kg) weight with a wing loading of not more than 22 pounds (10 kg) per square metre. It may carry up to two persons and must conform to a strict code of airworthiness. There are three categories of microlight – The Flexwing, The Three-Axis Controlled, and The Hybrid. The type which we chose for the purpose of our venture is of the flexwing range, based upon the design of a hang-glider, and controlled by the method known as weight shift. The controls are very similar to those of a hang-glider but this type of microlight has a wheeled trike suspended from it and a propeller at the rear driven by a small engine. Our choice was a Puma Sprint and in this model the pilot straps himself into a seat with a hang-glider-type horizontal bar in front of him with which he manoeuvres the wing, above which is a stabilising fin. A passenger can be carried, sitting in tandem behind the pilot.

The micro-light operator has a throttle and can control the direction of the front wheel with a small foot bar. It is basically a wheeled vehicle for land/air operations. Of particular interest to me was the fact that the Puma Sprint had already been tested with skis for working over snow and some trials had been made with floats. The important change in concept which derived directly from my original idea was to use the microlight with two-man floats, substantial enough to carry a pilot and passenger and to adapt the undercarriage in such a way as not only to accept floats and to carry spare kayaks and other equipment, but also to be easily interchangeable from float to wheel, to ski and vice versa.

The method of use I envisaged, was to have a light-weight machine which could be adapted to travel on water, on land, and in the air and then, when not required, could be readily disassembled for transporting. Such a concept would give a hitherto undreamed of dimension to exploration. Gone was the need for slow and frustrating scouting marches to ensure safety of men, kayaks and rafts. Gone the hazard of crevasse and fissure, waterfall and rapid, because our microlight would become the eyes of our expedition – our 'firefly scout'.

Needing a much shorter runway than a conventional plane, its use for carrying lightweight cargo such as kayaks and small stores would be invaluable to a highly mobile expedition. Its cheapness both in capital outlay and in the economy of maintenance and running costs would make it attractive in comparison with conventional planes and helicopters but above all, its facility for being put to rest, its wing folded, to glide downstream upon a raft, made it quite the best choice of vehicle for our particular expedition.

Sometime after we had interested Gerry in the project but before he was totally committed to our harebrained scheme, I met him at a Billiard Club near London. I explained the idea of the microlight using canoes as floats, but Gerry was not too happy about this. He explained 'A float is made in such a way as to have a "step" on the undersurface. As it gathers speed, it first of all "planes" almost on top of the water and then the "step" acts to lift it and break surface tension for take-off—I think you should start with a basic float design and convert *this* into a 'kayak'.

I thought about this—on face value it seemed logical, but in fact, it was not really a viable proposition. It old him, 'Yes Gerry, but just think about what a kayak has to do and the purpose for which it is designed. It has to roll, it has to swerve, tilt laterally and from front to back. It has to glide over water—and it does not have to take off—well not often anyway. I really can't see how we could do this with a float shape and especially with a step.' After considerable discussion I had to give up my idea of combining floats with kayaks and we decided to use floats as floats, which led us to a designer and maker of fast hulls, in the Isle of Wight.

There were many considerations in the concept of undercarriage adaptability. For instance, if we were thinking of adapting a microlight for water take-off then it must also be able to *land* on water. This statement seems obvious, but it really took quite a lot of thinking through to make it work for both. We had several meetings on this and similar subjects. Then we asked, could we take off from water and land on the ground? We talked of having wheels fitted inside floats, and of retractable wheels at the side of skis, for we had then come to realise that we needed three facilities for our three different terrains. Logic prevailed. In due course we worked out the actual logistics of our proposed journey (as far as we could at this stage) and were able to predict the various points at which we would need to change the undercarriage, and what these actual changes would entail. We knew when we would land on water and take off from grass or scrub and vice-versa. In the design of floats for flying, there had been a certain amount of work done for microlights to carry one person, and some successful models had been in use. As far as we knew, no one had ever succeeded in making two-man floats suitable for a pilot and a passenger and as our intention during the expedition was to have the ability to carry a passenger, it was a prerequisite of any design that it should fill the requirement of a two-man float. Martyn Levi, who owned 'Go Plane' at Gosport, Isle of Wight, promised to design and fabricate these in time for the expedition (his father, Sonny Levi, is a renowned designer of fast boat hulls). We were confident that with Martyn's knowledge and the back up of his father's skills we should soon have a prototype to test out. And it would be a 'First'.

But the design was not free of problems. When a propeller approaches 3000 r.p.m the tips of the blades are moving through the air almost at the speed of sound. Water droplets at this speed like steel balls, drawn from the wet ends of floats, could be very dangerous and could actually damage the propeller. A way to attach a water guard, fixed separately to the microlight frame, had to be found and this had to be consistent with flight and streamlining. 'How do we steer?' Rudders were then fitted to each float, connected by cables to levers operated by the pilot's feet. The first of these were to prove too small and to bring near disaster to one of our Puma Sprint microlights during Press Day at Reykjavík. We eventually fitted larger ones, which worked well. The day dawned when a pair of floats was ready for us to test, and as ITN television were interested and wanted preliminary footage before the expedition, we invited them to watch. We were excited—this was testing time—we knew that the idea was in its crude form but we also knew that the success of the innovation was crucial to the success of our expedition.

We contacted Ken Watson of Avon Inflatables who were to become major sponsors of Iceland Breakthrough and asked him to join us. Accordingly, Gerry, Mick, one or two others and I took a van and trailer (carrying the dismantled microlight and some canoes) to meet with Martyn Levi at his house in Gosport. We decided to give the whole set up a full test in the sea off the Isle of Wight, with microlight, floats, kayaks and raft.

* * *

Here it might be timely to offer some information about our choice of kayaks for the expedition. The terms CANOE and KAYAK are interpreted quite loosely in England, and insofar as the text of this book is concerned, I have occasionally used both words when referring to our craft. However, from a technical point of view, what we used were kayaks. In a canoe, we kneel and use a single-bladed paddle. In a kayak, we sit, using double-ended blades. Historically the canoe stems from the Canadian Indian, while the kayak derives from the Eskimos.

For our expedition we chose single-seater kayaks because we were expert in this field. With some fifteen or so years experience of kayaks, I felt that they were the ideal *probe* for the expedition. (The technique proper that we envisaged for the journey was three pronged—micros in the air, kayaks on the water and rafts as converters and carriers.) The single kayak is like a salmon in the river, it is responsive, it can stop easily, and it can dart about which makes it ideal for rescue work and for speedy reconnaissance. We needed large 'boats' shaped to withstand the immense pressure of rough water, with carrying space for emergency equipment and survival aids, but they had to be highly manoeuvrable, fast in a straight line, light enough to be airlifted, with strong 'spines' to stand up to use as sledges, and of high grade manufacture. We unanimously chose Olymp 5 which proved brilliant. From my earlier exploits on the Alsek in Alaska and the film we brought back, it had become obvious that from a safety aspect and also for the best results in picture making, the kayaks should be red. So each of our Olymps was supplied in that colour and each was personalised in such details as the foot rests, seats and so on.

Common to all of them was a safety set-up we had designed consisting of a toggle at each end (not a loop which is dangerous in rough water rescue work). A V-shaped cord extended from the stern to quick-release clips just behind the cockpit, on the deck, so that a swimmer could grab hold of one. The quick-release system made the rope available for towing. Forward of the cockpit, set transversely across the deck was an elastic strap, through which a paddle could be thrust while the kayakist's hands were occupied elsewhere, as for instance, in emptying a colleague's kayak. I was particular about the specification of these measures and they proved to be very effective in practice.

The kayaks were jammed full of buoyancy aids. A central column 4 inches to 6 inches wide ran centrally fore and aft of the cockpit from bows to stern and on the sides were four air bags. The object of this was to ensure that in a serious capsize, the amount of water filling in the kayak would be minimal. In rocky rapids a waterlogged kayak can smash very easily. The shapes of kayaks are many—like fishing rods, they are things of beauty and personal choice. But there are theories which govern design and they are briefly based on the following principles. A cylindrical kayak gives rigidity with lightness, and the 'flatter' it is in shape, the weaker it will be; shape in this instance, being involved with hull performance and streamlining, has a great effect upon speed and manoeuvrability. A V-shaped hull cuts through the water faster, but makes turning more difficult than a 'flat' hull. A flatter shape is slower in a straight line but more manoeuvrable. There is an interplay between all design shapes and their performance, one design leading to another—but with some balancing between shapes, it is possible to achieve stability, manoeuvrability and speed. Achieving this is very much an art form, and the man must be tuned to his craft.

Our Olymp 5s were the ultimate design in terms of a craft for broad wild rivers. Made impeccably by a company called Gaybo, they were strong, light, and very beautiful. The cockpit lips were especially large offering a good grip for the spray decks, the seat was well designed allowing fitting out to individual requirements, and the quality of workmanship was of the highest. The evolved size of 4 m in length, worked out that an average person would have a certain 'wetted' area in flat water. They were 60 cm side to side at centre line and 30 cm deep from 'keel' to deck. The material used was Diolin/Koulor (fibreglass), at the time the best and lightest combination. Today, however, there is movement towards plastic-moulded kayaks with better designs and lighter models—and as they rarely break they could be a real alternative for future expeditions. Ours had been designed in 1971 by a man called Klaus Lettmann and are universally accepted as an excellent kayak.

At Christmas 1982 Mick and I, together with some friends, went to Austria for some ski training. One day we found ourselves in a cable car, on our way to the top of a ski slope. We were talking of canoes, and sitting just opposite us in the car was a bearded Germanic gentleman. 'Excuse me' he said, 'I overheard your conversation—I too am interested in canoes . . .'

'Really?' Mick replied.

'Yes—my name is Lettmann.'

Mick's eyes opened wide—'Not one of the Lettmann family?'

'I am Klaus—Klaus Lettmann' was the reply.

We could hardly believe our ears—here we were sitting opposite the great designer of our favourite kayaks! We spent the next three days with him, skiing, talking of white water and canoe design and drinking a considerable amount of Schnapps. Life is enriched by such coincidences and it has lasted in our memory.

* * *

But to return to the Isle of Wight—the afternoon found us with the microlight on the gravel shore and four of us manhandling it to remove the wheels and to attach the new, shiny, white floats. The operation was not all that easy but eventually our Puma was gently launched into the sea, where she floated serenely in a calm bay. The day was sunny, it was spring, things looked good and we couldn't wait to start. The raft came out alongside and Mick and I, in our kayaks, paddled out into the bay. Wearing a crash helmet suitable for kayaking and flying, I nosed up to the microlight, climbed out of my boat very gingerly and strapped myself into the Puma, while someone else claimed my kayak. Then we took off—it was terrific—no problems, a smooth glide followed by a rising plane on water, and then separation and lift off. ITN filmed it, the very first time (except for works' prototype testing) that a microlight with two-man floats had taken off from water . . . we were *official!*

The camera crew were fascinated, and called for more shots, from different angles. Mick wanted to have a go, so he took my place in the passenger seat. Gerry was in love with this new toy and we flew and flew and landed and took off—and the minutes ticked by un-noticed.

'God, we're going to miss the ferry,' said a member of the ITN crew, 'and this film is supposed to be shown tonight in the studio in Southampton!'

We all looked at each other in consternation—but Gerry, forever cheeky and raring to go, said 'Don't worry, chaps—I'll fly it there!' We packed up the film in two aluminium boxes, which I strapped as firmly as I could to my stomach, climbed into some warm clothes and, having arranged to meet the others two or three hours later (they would take the late night ferry) we started the engine and with increasing speed, we lifted from the surface and gradually climbed to about 1000feet travelling northwards towards Southampton. It was a superb flight and we were charged with excitement. The television company were astounded to see us coming in to land in a small river estuary close to the side of the studio. We slowed the propeller and gently steered through the calm water to tie up along-side. I disembarked, ran in and handed the films with a proud flourish to the producer of the Evening News Programme. 'I believe you've been waiting for this!' I said, dripping all over his carpet. I don't remember his reply for, of a sudden, all hell was let loose—reporters came from all quarters to film the plane and to talk to us and to supplement the film, which by courtesy of our modern version of Wells Fargo went out to the British public that very night.

Microlights are useful things . . .

Expeditions Cost Money

We have talked of how we accumulated and stored equipment. Much of this came from our sponsors and it is of them and our fund raising efforts that I now write. Raising funds for an expedition is an art form! First comes the idea—then you take it a bit further to see if it really is practicable, then you make up a preliminary brochure— you lay out your aims and you show how you intend to achieve them. Then you make the point that this venture will achieve many firsts and establish records, which leads to the fact that you are in a position potentially to offer publicity. And so you go to your prospective 'customer' and tell him what you need and what you can do for him in return.

It is a hard climb—many refusals can weaken resolve. I always think it is rather like trying to climb a spiral staircase through a many-storied house, when some of the treads are rotten and may give way. You pretend that you are already half way up before you start, and it's only the will to reach the top which enables you to leap across the weak steps and continue climbing. But, find a weak step and it can pitch you down several floors—as evidenced by the problems which arose when a contract with a major TV company was turned down by us, only three weeks before take-off day. This was a matter of incompatibility and some personal difficulties, but it cost us several thousand pounds and dropped us at least three floors in our climb to the top, although we were, and still are, sure this was the right decision.

We had spent months trying to work through the medium of advertising agencies and public relations firms, with some direct approaches as well. Our method was to obtain the *Advertisers Year Book,* and then to approach an agency, asking for the name of the person in charge of the particular company's advertising account that we wished to speak to. We would then outline our proposed expedition and suggest to the agency that they put forward our package of several options in the nature of publicity to be gained from the venture to their customer(s). On the whole, this method did not result in much success, probably for two reasons. Firstly, I had rather misread the amount of time required for this type of approach to be effective. Many firms have a twelve or even eighteen-month planning cycle, and here was I asking in January for results before July.

Secondly, we encountered the condition I call 'The Below Line Syndrome'. Stated clearly, it became obvious that advertising agencies were not all that keen to put up proposals from outside their own organisations. Whatever the reasons for this reluctance, and they may have been more logistical than 'doctrinal' the fact remains that this avenue was somewhat barred. The public relations firms were more open to our advances and in some instances were very helpful in obtaining responses from their customers. But on the whole, the results were very disappointing. We had spent three months sending out our brochure, with a covering word processor letter and then following these up with many, many phone calls, all directed to a specific person in the organisation, the name of whom would have been the result in itself of much time-consuming research. We also at this time made approaches to companies found in the *Times 1000* which is a list of 1000 top companies, and to those firms dealing with specialised products which fell naturally within our field of endeavour.

By mid February, we were still considerably short of target and it was becoming increasingly obvious to me that I had to change tactics. The major part of £80,000 was still required and we had less than six months to find it.

It was then that I decided to make a more personal approach and to direct it towards firstly magazines and then film and/or TV companies, on the premise that while ordinary companies might be somewhat reluctant to venture money on the chance of having some stickers, some photos and some press coverage, a magazine would be likely to have interest in putting forward a story with pictures. And if so, then how much more would a film company be interested in having a film, with all its attendant spin-off publicity. So I offered the story with pictures to magazines and the film with story to film producers. Among the production companies were World Wide from England and Astrophore in France. World Wide became so enamoured of the project, they actually departed from precedent and offered sponsorship themselves. *Figaro* magazine became interested and we offered them French rights. ITN then were approached and bought world rights. And then my friend 'snowball' took over—news got around that we had something going and firms who thought video might suit them offered help, and as the snowball rolled faster and faster in came the funds and promises and contracts we had so desperately needed. But if it sounds easy, do not be lulled into complacency.

Increasingly, sponsorship is moving into this sophisticated, fairly new audio-visual area, where an expedition can offer to set up a wide variety of media coverage from its stills and filming, to a prospective 'investor'. The use of 'logos' and 'stickers' can be attractive to certain companies and we in fact did use some names on our equipment. A certain amount of discrimination must be used on this side of the advertisement machine as many countries have rather strict rules about the application of so called 'blatant' advertising. The successful entrepreneur will do his homework on these before 'selling his ideas'. Much of our sponsorship was in the form of goods, and some complications arose. For instance we had a technical problem with the sleeping bags from 'Ultimate'. I wasn't quite sure of the size, thickness and other specifications that would be best for us. After discussions with them, we settled for a certain model, but when later we tested these out in Scotland, we found that they were not warm enough for our purpose. There was then something of a panic on, but Ultimate came up with the goods and let us have a completely new stock of much heavier duty sleeping bags. These did not arrive until we were on our way to Iceland! The story of their travels until they finally met up with us the day before we went up on the glacier was almost worthy of an Iceland Saga . . . they were picked up by someone in Iceland, passed through customs, transported to a small hotel 'The Family House', in Reykjavík, where our good friends Erlingur and Andrea packed them and sent them on to Höfn, where somehow or other we finally got possession of them. Our grateful thanks go to Ultimate and to our many 'links in the chain'.

I remember how, in its usual style, our expedition took over people's houses with boxes. 'The Family House' was one such which suffered from our invasion. It was quite exciting (for us) when looking through fifteen or twenty boxes, we would find a whole load of crunchy bar biscuits ordered weeks ago in one box, balaclavas with gloves, socks and specially-made inner socks in another, a load of beautifully-made orange-coloured SP 27 jackets, all brand new and in different sizes in another. And yet another full of Alafoss sweaters. It was very much like opening up Christmas presents and we all whooped with delight at each new treasure we uncovered. It is great to recall that we eventually received everything (and more) that we had been promised and that apart from one or two minor hitches about sizing and specification everything went well. Our sponsors were magnificent in catering to our complicated requirements.

The team had of course, never been all together at one place. When we finally had all this gear, we had to distribute it, which we did at Gudbrandur's house. I put fifteen sets of everything into parcels: balaclavas, gloves, jackets SP 27, Ozee suits, leg warmers. Damart tops, goggles and other things besides . . . it was like a supermarket full of brand new clothes. Each person could select just what sizes he wanted, and considering the complications of getting all this arranged, each team member ended up very well kitted out.

Not every item of clothing was central to the expedition—for instance, the Alafoss sweaters. We would not normally reckon to use these on an expedition, although as it happened they did come in very useful during an exceptional storm. The idea of taking these was to have some publicity photographs of team members wearing them. Icelandic sweaters are a major industry in this rugged country and there is a link between our 'Outdoor Life' activity and the image sought by Alafoss. Mick and Jeb posed in these against an icy background. They also make very good presents . . . everyone treasures a beautiful Icelandic Sweater.

Not every sponsor relates to the expedition in direct terms—there are many companies whose products have nothing whatsoever to do with expeditions in particular, but where a connection suitable for publicising (and thereby gaining sponsorship) may be found. One such was World Wide Pictures Ltd. who sponsored post-production facilities for the film. Another was Victor Sumner & Co Ltd. who supplied the expedition with beautiful ties bearing our own Logo. Others had a more direct link, such as Olís oils. They became one of our major sponsors, giving us thousands of pounds worth of goods, in terms of oils and diesel and they also lent us two vehicles for the entire duration of the expedition. They were of tremendous assistance to us during our travels and we felt we had o do a lot of publicity for them, to repay their efforts. We took some film for them which was to give them the facility to produce a television advertisement when the Iceland Breakthrough film was released. We also carried logos, although as I've mentioned before, these were restricted to comply with advertising regulations. We were able to solve this problem in certain instances by applying stickers and logos for still photographs and then removing them during moving films.

Another sponsor who was of great importance to us was Icelandair, who gave us thousands of pounds' worth of help in the shape of all the free tickets we needed, not only to get the team in and out of Iceland, but all the tickets we needed to get the team around Iceland with internal flights. Icelandair has a logo 'Iceland—rugged but friendly'—at the end of our adventures, we simply had to agree the truth of this! We had stickers fixed showing this and these have since appeared in the press over a wide circulation and we believe, that Icelandair are happy with this and that our reputation has been that 'we deliver the goods' in terms of repayment of sponsorship by publicity. The Höfn Co-op were also generous in giving us free provisions.

There is always the intervention of luck, as evidenced by the story of 66° North. We undertook to stop where the river crosses the exact latitude of 66 degrees north and there to put up some plaques in front of which the team would be photographed wearing the clothing provided by this little company. In spite of our many difficulties which will be recounted in the story of the expedition proper, we managed to honour the intention and Robert took some excellent photographs. Providence was to step in again for the company when their pictures were inadvertently sent to *Figaro* magazine and were used in an article about the expedition.

We were delighted with all the food, clothing and equipment our sponsors provided to say nothing of the facilities laid on in Iceland and while I have mentioned in detail a few of them, there is one more that must be included. Honda supplied us with a portable generator to enable us to charge up batteries and to run our pieces of powered equipment. This really proved its worth when we were stranded on a glacier at a temperature of minus 30 deg. C, and it enabled us to weld together some broken equipment. This sturdy piece of machinery was quite impervious to outside influences, as we found when in another incident one of our vehicles reversed over it, crushing it into the ice. After we had dug the Honda out, and scraped off most of the ice, despite its somewhat distorted shape, it started once again at the very first pull. When we reported this to Honda, they glowed with pride!

We considered that in the main we were treated with kindness and enthusiasm by our sponsors and we hope that we were able to offer them the publicity they wished for, in return. To them we say a warm thank you—a list of all sponsors is shown in the acknowledgements.

Leaving Home—'Iceland Breakdown?'

Three days before our departure, everyone in our team, except the Icelanders, Jeb the rafter, and Gerry and Simon the fliers, found their way to my home at Hendon. In addition to myself there were Bruno, Benoit, Mick, Jean Jacques, and Jean-Luc. Also around at that time were my mother and father (Jack and Muriel) and my brother Jonathan. A constant stream of visitors flowed through our rooms, all of them having at some time or another had something to do with getting the expedition on its way and all coming to wish us good luck, god speed and safe return. Each and every one of them had in his or her own way smoothed our path. Between talking to visitors, scoffing great quantities of Mum's food, and even greater quantities of Dad's liquor, we could hardly find time to get the packing done—but gradually it came to order, and the various bedrooms became less chaotic, the number of mislaid goods reduced and there was a gradual shift of packed-up goods from the upper reaches of the house down towards what can only be described as the despatch department, an area of the drive bounded on one side by an outhouse (named Caesar's Palace, in memory of our pet goat who was a local favourite for some seventeen years till he died in 1979), and on the other side by the garden path leading to a large barn, in which an assortment of our larger stores was held. On the lawn itself was a partly dismantled microlight, with spars and rigging strewn about. Mum and Dad decided that they could not let the time go without having a party, so Dad booked a table at an Italian Restaurant in Belsize Park for about sixteen or so of our team and assistants. We had a wonderful evening and they produced a cake with a model of a microlight and a kayak on it, with the words 'Good Luck—Iceland Breakthrough' iced on the cake. We were in very high spirits and excited at the thought that after months and months of planning and working, we were about to turn the dream into the fact. The icing on the cake—would it lead us to the ice in the caves? And where would our wings and paddles take us—to the moon-scaped banks of Jökulsá á Fjöllum? We breathed a prayer that the luck which had been with us so far would favour us all the way.

The party went on until the small hours and then we were home, and rising soreheaded but early none the less, threw ourselves into the business of loading the convoy, fortified as we worked by a never ending stream of sandwiches. We had planned carefully and in particular, I had taken pride in the meticulous checking of every possible point which could have arisen — nothing, absolutely nothing had been left to chance, Except, . . . except, I must have had a blind spot about transport. What we should have had was a pantechnicon to take all our gear with Mick and Robert up to Newcastle for the ferry, and then to transport the rest of us, with the smaller items of equipment, up to Mallaig in the West of Scotland, where we were to embark on *Goodbye Girl*. What we actually had was a ramshackle hotch-potch of ill-assorted vehicles—a VW Van belonging to Robert, with a hired trailer attached (the trailer's lights were inoperative and we had to do a rewiring job before setting off). Next we had my old Renault 5 which was in moderate condition, and my even older Renault 4 van, which could be quite easily identified through the layers of rust and batter. Jean-Luc put his old Renault 4 into the kitty and it made a wonderful start to the expedition. We had said emotional farewells to everyone at the gate of Model Farm House, Hendon and two hundred yards up the hill, Jean-Luc's exhaust (the car's actually!) fell off. We returned shamefacedly down the hill and spent an hour wiring the thing back into place. We had one other vehicle—a week before the departure date, I had bought a Blue Hillman car for £275. To this we attached Dad's boat trailer, which was rather heavy and tended to lift the car off the ground until we stabilised it with weights in the back seat and boot. Converting the trailer for carrying chests and assorted equipment was mind boggling. My father, who had spent almost five years as a Royal Marine during World War 2, rather thought he knew more about knots than we explorers and insisted on giving us lessons in the making of lorrymen's hitches and the like. We found boards which we tied on and fixed together, and then we lashed boxes on to them and the edifice grew higher and higher. We roped and roped and revised and revised. Dad tied, Benoit untied, Dad lashed, Robert

48 relashed. Mick and Dad (both from the Marine mould) then got together and fixed everything securely—and after that nothing came adrift.

The Start

We were off. Slowly, as slow as the worst vehicle among us (and it would be hard to say which this was) we proceeded up the M1, five rather tired cars carrying seven rather tired but exhilarated would-be-explorers. At some point approaching level with Newcastle, Mick and I separated from the main convoy to go to Ultimate Equipment, who had arranged for sleeping bags and tents to be left in a small garage adjoining one of their directors' houses. We picked them up at about 1.00 in the morning and returned to the convoy—but we couldn't—it had moved!

Our arrangement to meet them at a certain motorway service station had fallen through because we had used a road map with old notation on it, and it appeared that a new motorway extension had since been built and that the numbers of various roads had been changed. By some miracle, and after several back-tracks, we all met at three o'clock and the rest of the team couldn't understand the meaningful glances thrown between Mick and myself.

We finally arrived at the Docks at Newcastle, and loaded up the major equipment, Customs officials stamped our comprehensive lists to save us re-importation duty. Meanwhile, I had realised that I had some phone calls to make and that I needed to photocopy some addresses for Mick, so I shot off into Newcastle. I made my calls and copied the papers and then went in search of some batteries which we needed to back up our gear just in case a promised consignment failed to materialise. And there, before my eyes, parked outside a tobacconist, in a street in Newcastle, I espied an Ever Ready van . . . the driver raised his eyebrows when I asked him for 300 batteries, but he had them on board and very soon we had them back at the docks just before Mick left.

What an omen! Now I knew—I knew that fate would smile on us for the rest of the expedition. And it did! Well, for most of the time anyway . . .

Right, top: **Becalmed in the middle of the North Sea.**

Right, bottom: **Bruno Cusa (back left), Benoit Dabout (back right), Bruno Bazin (middle), Marc Bizien (front left) and Paul Vander-Molen (front right) on** *Goodbye Girl.*

those on the low side.

Marc in his broken English called Stornoway Coast Guard—'Stoneway Coost Geerd—Mike Foxtrot Tango Lima, do you read, over?' Stornoway read him, but the English reply was too much for him and he asked me to take the phone. I leaned from my top bunk to grasp the receiver and was thrown to the other side of the cabin, landing heavily on Bruno Cusa who had at last moved into the cabin. He was unhurt, but as I came to a stop against the edge of a wooden chair I banged my left hip. The chair didn't mind—I did—it was quite painful. But I cheered up when I heard the lovely voice of the girl who answered Stornoway calls, and was about to get into stride on the radio when another lurch sent me hurtling to the deck. By the time I had picked myself up she had gone. My hip was now very painful and I began to wonder if it would affect my skiing. Even the two French skippers were not feeling too well and the awful movement seemed to be never-ending.

At about 5 o'clock, I took the helm with Marc. The wind had dropped, the sea had subsided and life was returning to normality. The others awoke around 9.00 and started to come alive. Apart from slight headaches, we felt well and downed copious draughts of warm liquid accompanied by choruses of 'Tea for Two'. Now with a tidy cabin, we could think straight and I estimated that we had about 300 nautical miles to go. On yesterday's logging we would have done that in about two days but now that the wind had dropped we were only averaging about one knot, and it was going to take much longer.

Becalmed

As the day progressed, the wind regressed—our one knot dropped to just a fraction and by the evening we were becalmed. Bruno-C threw an empty egg carton over board and three hours later it overtook us. The day wore on, and slowly the sun sank on the horizon. I was at the *barre*–the tiller. The sea was calm and the night sky clear. The others were resting and someone was preparing a meal in the galley. From my position in the stern I could see the after hatch leading to our accommodation, while on each side of the boat, just in front of me, were three lockers, upon which we could sit along the bulwarks. I was in reflective mood and thinking of what might lie ahead. My reverie was disturbed by a call of *'Encore des oeufs, s'il vous plait!'* from the galley.

The locker furthest forward from me on the port side did service as one of the many food stores, and I reached forward, still grasping the end of the tiller, to lift the lid. I put my hand inside to pick up a carton of eggs, and to my absolute horror felt something warm and fleshlike! I jumped back, nearly falling over the *barre* in my consternation, and then recovering myself, I leaned forward again to have another look. I saw a dismembered hand lying upon the boxes in the locker, and before my astonished gaze, the fingers started to move! They took hold of a carton and I saw the eggs and fingers slowly disappear through the side of the locker—I took a long slow deep breath and waited for my racing pulse to subside—and it was only then that I realised that the chef must have had an assistant and that there was a small hatch leading directly from the galley into this locker which was the larder. My reverie, so abruptly terminated, was lost beyond recall.

Overleaf, left: *Goodbye Girl* **becalmed. 'Bruno threw an empty egg carton overboard and three hours later it overtook us.'**

Overleaf, right, top: **Gerry and Paul practising take-off and landing with kayaks attached to the microlight, over the lake.**

Overleaf, right, bottom: **The second raft was fitted with a rowing frame built by Jeb; it's seen here loaded with two of the kayaks.**

The Sea Crossing

On the evening of 20 July 1983, just seven months after my meeting with Mick, we packed all we could into our tiny boat *Goodbye Girl* and set sail for Iceland. The 34-foot (10-m) sloop had two 'cabins' up forward. These were completely filled with medical gear, camera equipment and personal luggage. The toilet, situated between the two front bunks and the main cabin was also full, being the repository of three large orange fenders and the spinnaker. The main cabin was situated towards the stern; it was a box 6 feet high, 11 feet long and about 6 feet wide (2 m x 3 m x 2 m). In this we were to live for several days—live, cook, eat, sleep, dream, navigate, take soundings and talk of our plans. Under the bunks and in every conceivable locker, cupboard or hole, we had packed food.

We formed ourselves into three watches and in mild weather sailed away. The wind was slight at first and it seemed to take years for the Isles around us to disappear into the distance. The sea remained calm for two days but gradually the wind started to increase, and slowly became strong enough for the spinnaker to send us sailing along. We were visited by dolphins and Bruno thought he saw a whale, but apart from this, the journey so far was uneventful. To pass the time usefully, Marc Bizien and Bruno Bazin (Bruno-B), the skippers, gave us a lesson in 'position find' and we learned how to take the *'barre'*, the tiller. I shared a watch with Bruno-B, Jean Jacques was in Marc's watch and Bruno Cusa (Bruno-C), Benoit and Jean-Luc formed the third.

The spinnaker, so brightly coloured, was a sight to behold with the sun glowing between clouds. Islands became lit up with artistic light reflected from the sea and Bruno-C, inspired, started filming while Jean-Luc took stills, and Jean Jacques recorded sound amid a jumble of sails, ropes and pulleys.

On the third day the sea became choppy and we felt rather sick. Bruno-C, the cameraman, sat rolled up in a ball on the stern deck unable to move with nausea. For twenty-four hours he stayed there as waves rolled over the boat and smashed down onto his body. His numerous layers of thermal clothing contrived to keep him warm.

I awoke in the cabin . . . was it day or night? The boat heaved around all over the place and as I hid my head under my sleeping bag I heard water come crashing in. I hurriedly dressed. The surrounding sea had become transformed, mounds of water were rolling towards the side of the boat and our small box cabin was pitching forward and backward and sideways. I took the helm with Bruno-B and discovered just how difficult it is to keep a boat on a steady bearing as it rides the crest of a wave, dips into the trough and slews round off course.

By midday every one of us (except the skippers) had been sick. The boat became a mess. It was impossible to move and we stayed either lying in our bunks or at the helm. Jean Jacques lost his smile and looked somewhat like a drunken bulldog, while I, feeling awful, took some Alpen and water so that I could at least have something to bring up. The sleeping arrangements in the cabin were based upon lower bunks which became daytime seat lockers, above which was a canvas rolled on a bar which converted into an upper 'hammock' when the bar was located between two wooden brackets. It had been specifically designed, we thought, to allow those sleeping on the high side to fall out onto

Morning came, but still the sea remained calm and the air still. Apart from fish and an occasional sea bird we had seen no signs of life since we set off, but now, drifting somewhere between Scotland and Iceland, we found ourselves heading towards a small vessel which appeared in the distance. Keen to establish our position, we made radio contact: 'Icelandic Fishing Trawler *Bordones* 60 deg 24 min North—9 deg 15 min West' came the reply. We were twenty miles further south-east that we had calculated—we had in fact moved slightly away from Iceland. We were frustrated—the sea was still. The only movement was the sea gulls, soaring and then skimming just a millimetre above the surface, with black tipped wings outlined against the sparkle of white light, as gracefully they dipped and turned in their never ending search for food.

The enforced inactivity allowed us to get rather more civilised about our eating and sleeping arrangements and we managed to have some quite reasonable meals. Friction, inevitable among men in such confines, was remarkably little and small bursts of irritation were quickly dissipated by the general good humour. Bruno-C, although serious from time to time, was ever ready for a good laugh and Jean Jacques, with his subtle sense of humour kept us amused. Benoit, the youngest among us, perhaps felt the frustration a little more keenly than the others and like me, longed for the freedom of a kayak. Jean-Luc was not entirely cheerful. We thought that he was unhappy about some of his photographic equipment, but the problem, whatever it was, seemed to resolve itself and, on the whole it was a happy band of explorers who awoke on the fourth day out to a bacon and eggs breakfast, a moving sea, wind in the right direction and an increasing speed of 3 to 4 knots.

In the afternoon, up spinnaker and we were cleaving the waves at 6–7 knots. Our spirits soared at the thought of reaching Höfn the next day, which now began to look a distinct possibility. But then we had other problems—the toilet became blocked—and refused to get itself unblocked in spite of vituperation and insults directed at it by Jean-Luc (in French of course). He vented his frustrations on the pump, the bowl and all concerned parts, quite unprintably, but cheered up considerably when we played back a recording of his monologue, taken secretly! The toilet, however, stubbornly refused to move. We of course had to move—bodily functions wait for no such convenience as a working toilet, and so we had to devise a way. Minor functions were not difficult, provided one checked the wind direction, but for major evacuations we had to climb to the forepeak of the craft with a harness beneath our clothes, then remove some of our clothes, place our feet behind one of the forward rails and lean over. Both hands were required for balance, so that teeth had to be brought into play to hold the toilet paper. It was cold, it was wet. On film it *is* funny but in practice you can't laugh . . . remember you have the paper in your mouth!

So we sped forward towards Iceland. We had nothing spectacular to record on film—nothing that is that could be shown to the public! But now the sky darkened, and the rain came—not heavily but drizzling and penetrating. I was damp through after my second watch. We took the spinnaker down but our speed was steady at about 6 knots. We were on course 345 deg. North. Inside everyone relaxed, Benoit was sleeping on the map table, while Jean-Luc, Jean Jacques and Bruno-C dozed off the effects of potatoes, cabbage and tinned sausages. At the table I filled in my diary. It was 15.36 in the afternoon of Sunday 24th July, our fourth day at sea, and reading it again now it tells me that we had not much food left, the toilet was still blocked, we were on to our reserve water supply and we were not going very fast. But it tells too that spirits were high, anticipation keen and that the atmosphere was good. On our fifth day we saw the coast of Iceland. And then slowly we bore towards the small, southern port of Höfn.

We tied up alongside a jetty and two customs officials came aboard. Our papers had been settled some months ago and all was in order. Marc signed papers and we gave them some tea, after which they left . . . perhaps it *was* the tea! We stepped ashore, in Iceland at last!

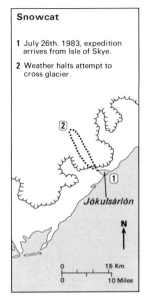

Snowcat

1 July 26th. 1983, expedition arrives from Isle of Skye.

2 Weather halts attempt to cross glacier.

Jökulsárlón

N

0   15 Km
0   10 Miles

Arrival At Iceland

Press Day

We had arranged a Press Day in Reykjavík 250 miles (400 km) to the west of Höfn, for the 27th of July. We met up with Gísli and Gudbrandur, our Icelandic team members, and boarded the plane for the coastal city. We landed at Reykjavík and for the very first time the whole team met together. We exchanged stories—Gerry Breen, our microlight pilot had arrived that morning from Luxembourg. He had just completed the French Grand Prix Race and was badly shaken—two of his friends had been killed in the race. Jeb Stuart, our rafter, had driven across America for forty-eight hours, virtually non stop, and had only just made his flight from Chicago. Mick and Robert had arrived with the main equipment which they had brought over in the ferry and were now with us.

The plane was to take our specially designed microlight down to the harbour and show the world for the very first time how this machine could take off from the water carrying either the pilot and a passenger or the pilot with some equipment. As we made our preparations hundreds of people began to arrive. The national newspapers sent their reporters, the radio sent their interviewers and a TV camera crew arrived with full equipment. Everyone waited expectantly as we took the machine down to the water's edge and the excitement grew as we replaced the wheels of the microlight with our specially-designed floats.

We had many sponsors, so we had agreed to take one person from each of the companies for a flight around the harbour. The first to go was a girl from the airline, Icelandair, who had been so helpful to us. She climbed aboard, looking beautiful and contriving to remain elegant. Gerry motored gently towards a suitable take-off area but the wind, which had been picking up somewhat, blew him off course. The rudders apparently were not effective with this sort of cross wind and he tried in vain three times to reach the open water. The crowd started to murmur—they were becoming anxious. 'What's going on?' we heard someone say, 'What's wrong? Why does it take so long?' Long minutes passed and then one of the safety boats which had been circling the harbour, reversed towards Gerry and threw him a line. As he leaned down to catch it the wind caught the tip of the wing, and Gerry, passenger and microlight toppled slowly and painfully over, on top of Benoit who, at that time was hovering near in his kayak. A cry went up and the crowd rushed over to the site of the accident. I called for everyone to get back and five members of the team raced over to Gerry who was trapped upside down in the capsized machine. The girl from Icelandair was made of stern stuff and reappeared, wet, but in complete command of herself and gained everyone's admiration.

The media descended on us clamouring for explanations. 'Oh—that's nothing—this sort of thing happens all the time' we told them. 'The floats are built so strongly it will be OK once we get it up.' We don't know if they really believed us. The people on shore looked shocked and Mick and I set to the job of trying to calm things down. The crowd were amazed and no less were we, when we quickly righted the machine, and, having

Left, top: **The 'ski run', one of the numerous tongues of ice that fall from the mighty ice cap in a steep progression to the lake. When we finished our testing and training period, we climbed this using the Snowcat, skiddoos and skis in our attempt to cross the glacier.**

Left, bottom left: **'Huge blocks of ice crash from the extremity of the glacier and directed by wind and current sail in galleon splendour around and across the water.'**

Left, bottom, top right: **Mick Coyne manoeuvring his kayak through the icebergs. The red 'pogies' on the paddle are fixed mittens for use in more turbulent waters.**

Left, bottom right: **Gerry testing the floats on the microlight while other team members watch from the inflatable.**

checked for damage (of which there was none save a slightly bent fixing bolt) Gerry shook himself free of excess water and decided to try another take-off. This time, with full throttle on, he took the plane hard into a cross wind. Slowly she gathered herself then a little faster and faster still, rising on to the water's surface and into a planing attitude and then surging to full speed, she freed herself of the waters' clasp and, to wild applause, circled above us. Relief and happiness flowed through the team—we had done it and we'd given them a show.

But it wasn't over yet. Five minutes passed, Gerry was out of sight. Five more minutes and he had not returned. We waited, but still no sign of our pilot and now the watchers on the shore were becoming worried. The TV crew came to us again 'What's happening? Where's the plane?'

'He's probably had to land further up the harbour—the wind here may be too strong for him,' I guessed.

I saw out of the corner of my eye, the two rescue boats speeding off in the general direction in which Gerry had disappeared. My heart came into my mouth. What could have happened? Mick and I looked at each other, not bearing to think of the possibilities. As the crowd started to climb a nearby hill to try for a sight of the microlight, we heard the noise of the boat's engine and into our vision drew the microlight, on a tow line from the rescue boat. The micro's engine had seized and Gerry had been forced to make an emergency landing on the water further up the harbour.

The motor was started later without too much difficulty. The fault might have had something to do with the capsize earlier. But we had learned a lot from this showing—the rudders needed changing, the wind was a serious factor in waterborne take off and some other things besides.

And now it started to rain—we decided that enough was 'un oeuf' (one of our Anglo-French bon mots), and that we would cut the microlight display even though this deprived Gerry of the chance to fly the many lovely girls who had travelled down in the hope of a flight. So as not to disappoint the 150 people now remaining, we demonstrated formation kayak rolling in the harbour, and it was appreciated. The final word on the day goes to Jeb. We had arranged for stickers and suitable publicity material to be on show on our machines and equipment, as appropriate to the rules of sponsorship but Jeb certainly hit the nail on the head when he said in his rich Colorado accent 'Jeese—if we'd known she'd go upside down, we'd have put stickers on the bottoms of the floats!' Epitaph for lost opportunity. Malgré tout—in spite of everything, the day went well—the news report was great and diplomatically showed Gerry taking off, not taking water! And we closed our day with a delicious meal and much-needed sleep. Tomorrow we would go back to Höfn to prepare for the lake.

Training and Testing on the Lake

On the southern edge of the Vatnajökull glacier numerous tongues of ice fall from the mighty cap in a steep progression to the sea. At the base of one such tongue is situated a lake—Jökulsárlón. Huge blocks of ice crash from the extremity of the glacier and, directed by current and wind, sail in galleon splendour around and across the water.

Every now and then one of these ice sculptures finds the small river Jökulsá in the far south of the lake, and escapes into the sea.

Our plan was to spend a few days on this lake to practise our techniques, test equipment and to acclimatise ourselves to the conditions. But getting to the lake from Höfn wasn't quite as simple, nor as quick as we had thought. Meetings with the Life Saving Association, last minute shopping, checking gear, packing, repacking, getting our new sleeping bags, the final fixing of canoe racks, last minute additions of clothes and much more besides, all had to be done first. Mick had 'flu which did not make for speed, and I had a stiff neck—but somehow or other we managed to get everything slotted in and made arrangements for some filming work at the same time. Some minor problems arose to do with food provided for the return crew of the boat but this was soon sorted out, and, amid heavy rain, Höfn saw us working at full pelt.

Robert and Jean-Luc oversaw the food. Mick, the climbing, camping and cooking gear. Gísli, welder extraordinaire put together most things that had come apart, while Jeb, professionally a carpenter, who could turn his hand to almost anything practical, built a rowing frame for the second raft. We painted it yellow. In all this frantic activity, we hardly noticed the hours passing, nor the days becoming nights—but at the end, tired but happy, we went to bed on the night of Saturday 30th July, dreaming of a good early start at about 8 o'clock on the Sunday morning.

We climbed aboard our vehicles, stowing the last of our equipment and watched Gerry take off—and what a take off! Flying between houses and a barn, his wing tip dangerously close to a lamp post, he rose to clear the obstructions and Jean-Luc, his passenger, waved down at us. We, on the ground, travelled across a broken dirt track in one of our four-wheel-drive trucks. And as we arrived, the microlight flew over the water, the sun shone on the Jökulsárlón and in the distance Vatnajökull, half hidden by cloud, dominated the brilliant scene. We had not realised the beauty we would encounter, for the lake is a rich blue with, on its surface, exotic shaped ice sculptures designed by wind and element gliding in random state, occasionally catching glints from the elusive sun. We saw no fish, but at the entrance to the sea, seagulls soared and screamed in profusion, and played among the turrets and arches of the icebergs. On the black and grey gravel of the shore, diamonds of ice sparkled and signalled their joy of the reflected sun, and as our trials proved worthy, we responded to the scene with an excess of *joie de vivre,* for in the soul of every man who longs to travel nature's way there is a place for the love of beauty.

In the tongues of ice descending from the cap were huge crevasses, appearing black in the distance, zebra striping the wall of the lake, and in places looking, as Mick said 'like a well used ski run'. Gerry circled the lake and at the same time another light aircraft appeared and circled in the opposite direction and we watched this graceful aerial ballet. Cars arrived at the lake's edge, to watch, as Gerry came down to land. There to meet us, by good chance, was Tony Escritt, one of the people who had done so much for us in the early stages of organising the expedition. We offered him a ride in the microlight, but Gerry took me up first to scout the area. At 40 mph it was very, very cold and although I was grateful for my protective clothing, my ears were freezing and I wished I had worn a balaclava as well. Tony went up for his trip and meanwhile vans, cars, trucks of all descriptions were drawn up in serried ranks—it was amazing to see all this stuff at our disposal.

60   *Goodbye Girl* had arrived and was anchored 750 feet (250 m) out to sea. Several of the team went out in kayaks, rafts and Zodiacs (fast rescue boats from Iceland Lifesaving Association). We made several journeys unloading the boat and used the opportunity for some more filming. We got some superb aerial shots when Gerry with his mastery of aerobatics flew close to the boat with Bruno Cusa leaning precariously out of his seat to get the best camera angle. Gísli, meanwhile feeling it essential to test out the life jackets and wet suits, had decided to leap into the sea . . . which he did, and professed himself quite satisfied. Some half an hour or so later, he was with three of the others in a Zodiac when a wave caught them abeam, and he, unbalanced, toppled back into the water—much to his surprise! It was here that the value of our 'eyes' and 'ears' came to be appreciated—Gerry high above in the microlight, contacted us by radio, 'How many should there be aboard the Zodiac?' Gerry, sped to the rescue. Within seconds he was flying above the Zodiac to check if all was OK and radioed back to us that he had seen Gísli clamber aboard, to the great relief of all. It really brought home to us the great potential for safety and security offered by our all-seeing flying machine.

We set up an ad-hoc camp on the beach and just before 9 pm Gerry took several members of the team up in the air one by one, to admire the scene and for the thrill of flying over the lake . . . until finally, tired, we slept to the sound of surf on sand and the occasional gull's call.

Acclimatisation

The next day was spent dealing with our equipment, filming, getting last minute pieces from Höfn and working very, very hard. The team were full of zest and the atmosphere was buzzing. The kayaks required some kitting out to get them into the condition we required and Benoit set about this in no uncertain manner. Gísli had welded some brackets to the microlight so that skis could be attached (they were rather like the rowlocks on the raft). A carrying frame was made for the kayaks which was very flexible in use, and the floats were given a more effective rudder system. We also fixed a baffle to prevent the exhaust from damaging the kayaks in flight. In addition to a spare engine which we carried, we had ordered another reserve motor which would have to come from England. But Gerry was delighted with the microlight. Gudbrandur had given me some radio instruction in Höfn and I was keen to test out communications, which were very good. We had food, trucks and enthusiasm.

Gísli, exploring part of the lake, found an exciting hole in an iceberg and climbing through, attached ropes for practising—it was quite a sight to see and it proved a useful training device for our later exploration of the ice caves. On the morning of 2nd August, 1983 we fixed the kayaks on to the microlight. Gerry took off easily from the ground this time and a man from Iceland TV came to film this; the microlight carrying kayaks was another 'first' for us. We then moved our camp along the river closer to the lake, set up the microlight on floats and all went in for some strenuous water activities. We took two kayaks through ice berg holes, one pushing the other, in which a cameraman was tied, and obtained some amazing shots of the 'inside' of these incredible white and blue monuments. We worked on the rafts and spent much time loosening ourselves up and trimming our gear. Final adjustments to clothes were made and we all felt that testing time was approaching.

Damages

The microlight had been circling, and we noticed that Gerry was having difficulty in controlling its movement. We thought at first that the differing temperatures of cold air rising from the lake, meeting the warm surrounding air and causing severe turbulence was the reason, but after landing on the water, he had the utmost difficulty in getting airborne again. He was in the throes of his fourth or fifth attempt when, to our horror, he did an abrupt 90 degree turn and almost cartwheeled—something was seriously wrong! We hauled the bird from the water and examined the floats. The underside of one of them had been ripped open and it had taken on board a considerable volume of water. We realised how lucky he had been not to have an awful accident. Gerry reckoned it must have struck a small iceberg. 'Just like the Titanic' he said, with his ever present impish humour.

Gísli, Gerry and I went back to Höfn in a pick-up truck to see what could be done with the damaged float. Our nerves had been exposed by the potential for disaster, and they were now brought to fine pitch by the hair-raising driving of Gísli—*he* might have been used to the appalling road but Gerry and I were certainly not, and at high speeds we were scared stiff—but we got there and some eight hours of work saw the float in good order.

Meanwhile, back at the lake, the weather had changed. A warm front had been approaching in the early part of the day with light winds, but by tea time the wind had picked up, light drizzle was bathing the scene and stratus cloud rested on the mountain tops. There was a forecast of further deterioration and we were very concerned at the loss of possible flying time—the micro performed best in light airs and we wanted to get in as much training and acclimatisation as possible.

Gerry, Gísli and I returned to the lake—we would not need the floats for some days and we had still some preparations to complete. We found that in our absence the team had been filming and had, in spite of the worsening weather, taken some brilliant shots, using the Zodiac boat and kayaks. At about 9 pm we went to where our Snowcat was parked, near the lake's edge. The Snowcat is a large tracked vehicle, specially designed for the treacherous ice work of the glacier and on this one Gísli had worked throughout the spring to make a fine cabin in which we could shelter and which would hold some of our stores, both inside and on its roof. We got it loaded up and eventually, thoroughly tired, went to bed early.

We had been on the lake for several days and our work there was complete. Tomorrow we would begin to get the team onto the glacier.

Ski-Plane

The following morning, Gerry flew his microlight up above the glacier to scout the terrain ahead. He returned saying 'God—it's like World War Three up there!' and reported a surface badly scored with crevasses, many of them hundreds of metres in length and dangerously deep. It was obvious to us that we could not transport the microlight through the approach area on top of a trailer (as had been our intention) because of the danger from severe shaking, and it was equally obvious that Gerry could not land on the glacier with his wheels (which had now been put back, in the absence of the floats) should we decide to fly up to it. We sought another solution. The aerial scouting had shown that some portion of the glacier's surface beyond the crevassed area had appeared from the air to be smoother and covered in with a thick layer of snow. We had the excellent skis which we had made a few days earlier and the brackets Gísli had welded, so Gerry could land on the glacier with his skis. But first things first—we were based on an area of scrubland at the bottom of the glacier. How do you take off from scrubland with skis designed for landing and taking off on snow!

'I could take-off from land with these skis if we can find a runway area and clear it of stones and obstructions,' Gerry said.

'Can you do that? Have you done it before?' I asked.

'No—never been done as far as I know,' he replied, shrugging his shoulders and moving off to inspect the land.

After some searching we found a relatively smooth section of grassy earth and having removed some hummocks and rocks, rolled the micro into position. We took off the wheels and spent some time fixing the skis and carefully adjusting the tensioning ropes. These ropes were not the only thing to be tense—we were all wondering if this thing could be done, although Gerry showed no signs of nerves at all. To an onlooker the scene would have looked ridiculous—a microlight, fitted with skis, and not a single patch of snow in sight, rather like sitting in a boat on a dried up river bed waiting for the water to flow!

Gerry announced that he was ready. Bruno positioned himself to film and Jean-Luc ran to the end of our 'runway' to take a photograph of this first ever dry take-off on skis. Ignition, cough, fire, rotate and at three quarter throttle she was ready to move—but she would not move—she shuddered and strained but stuck fast. We watched Gerry trying desperately to jolt it forward using his body weight and at the same time throwing in full engine power. Suddenly she began to move. The acceleration was surprising once she was going and it was quite a sight to see Gerry and wings hurtling down the 'runway' and within 30 feet (10 m) taking to the air quite abruptly. In fact it was all so sudden it took Jean-Luc unawares at his station and he almost missed the photo.

Gísli, who had agreed earlier to go up onto the glacier with a skiddoo (one of our small snow bikes) and to wait for Gerry high up in the snow, was looking anxiously for his arrival, having in the meantime marked off obstructions and crevasses on the route with flags. But Gísli was to have a longer wait—for looking up at Gerry we saw that one of the skis had come adrift from its tension rope and was swinging upside down. He was fighting the ski with one hand and trying to control the machine with the other. To land like this would have been disastrous, and we watched agonised as he struggled. The rope had not completely disengaged and he was able to get the ski back into position for landing, although unable to secure it. Holding it down he slowly lost height and speed and came in to land, making the attitude of the plane change at the last minute so as to come down on the rear portion of the ski which was stable and then touching down smoothly. The sheer skill and courage of this man held our admiration.

Our breath back, and our nerves under some control we realigned the ski securely, repositioned the trike for another take-off and this time he went straight up into the air and forward to meet with Gísli on the snowline, far up the glacier.

The Glacier

The Vatnajökull glacier is majestic. She rules a vast dominion of rugged crests and crevasses, caverns and cascades. She is ever changing, with hidden life and movement within her icy heart and beware the traveller who takes her lightly.

The journey from the lake to the top of the glacier in our Snowcat took about ten hours. The zebra-striped crevassed area was much more rugged than we had imagined, and the Snowcat rose and pitched like a World War I tank in the trenches of the Somme—except that here there was no mud, but spectacular flows of water rushing in the depths of the iced surface through self-made channels and convoluted grooves, beautiful to behold but so very treacherous. Mountains flanked our left- and right-hand view and clouds appeared and disappeared, whisping up and over the peaks and plateaus.

The sun was hot—it was August and the Icelandic summer was in full bloom—or so we thought. The view behind us was glorious: there was the lake with its bergs and birds, and in the distance we could see the sea spanning from left to right and curving to embrace the horizon. The colours were so blue, for the weather had cleared—and all seemed fine with the world. We carried on and eventually, tired but in some way triumphant, we reached the snow line without much incident. We had almost lost one of our trailers in a crevasse but ingenuity and perseverance had brought it to the surface with little loss except our time and we were now ready to set up camp. Gerry and Gísli made their way separately to the rendezvous and for the first time we slept on the soft snow. We slept well all of us.

In the morning, we awoke in high spirits and started breakfast. I was settling down to some food, when I heard Gísli call me—'Here Paul, it's for you.' I looked at him—he was standing by the side of the Snowcat—and on a wire protruding from its window was a telephone receiver! Automatically I got up to take the call—to the vast amusement of the rest of the team. Gísli had brought the receiver with him all the way from Höfn, to the top of this vast Ice Cap, just to pull this prank. The team fell about. (During the course of organising the expedition, I had perforce to use the telephone frequently—so frequently that the rest of the team had noticed although until now no one had mentioned it!) I was immediately named 'Mr Phoney' and it stuck for the rest of the expedition.

When we had all stopped laughing, we finished breakfast and set to work on some repairs. The skis of the microlight had become damaged when Gerry made his way across the snow to join us—now using the microlight as a snow vehicle without its wing! It was surprisingly efficient and fast. Amazingly, up on the glacier, we were able to drill holes with power, and rivet pieces together for emergency repairs, all by courtesy of a superb piece of equipment—a portable Honda generator—our 'suitcase of electricity', as we called it. It always started without demur when required and resisted all attempts to destroy it. While Jeb, Gerry and I worked on the microlight and its gear, Gísli and some of the others repaired one of the wheel runners of the Snowcat. One of our skiddoos was a casualty and we decided to leave it at this first base camp.

By late afternoon we were ready to implement our plan to reach Oraefajökull, the highest mountain in Iceland on our way across the glacier.

The glacier has its own weather system—and it could change rapidly and dramatically almost without warning. The sun, which had cheered us on our climb and refreshed us when we awoke, now disappeared behind cloud—we would not see it again for five long days. The cloud descended and engulfed our convoy: the Snowcat loaded to its absolute maximum, pulling a large box trailer on ski runners, behind which was a crocodile of two small trailers, Gudbrandur on a skiddoo, Jean-Luc, Bruno and I in the rear of this on our skis with tow ropes from Gudbrandur and then, bringing up the tail, Gerry, his microlight now changed from a 'Puma' to a 'Snow Leopard' (with its wing safely stored aboard the Snowcat), the propeller gliding him forward on skis. All were engulfed by this cloud, and as the weather rapidly deteriorated our crocodile climbed aboard the Snowcat, leaving just Gerry and Gudbrandur in convoy. Visibility became less and less until it was almost zero and for hours we drove cautiously and very, very slowly ahead grateful for the flags which Gísli and Mick had earlier fixed to mark a route through a crevasse field. We passed safely through the marked area. The temperature dropped and the wind rose—it was now well below freezing point and the noise was building up.

'What do you mean, we're back where we started?' Gerry screamed at Gísli. 'I've been outside for four hours now and all you can say is we're back in the same place!'

The compass in the Snowcat had gone haywire and from the little we could see we really did seem to have come round in a circle. The blizzard was increasing in intensity every minute and we made the decision to move no further until we could at least see the ground ahead. We would have to make camp and wait for an improvement in the weather. Outside the Snowcat, the wind was blasting everything in its path. The ropes holding the canvas cover of the trailer had frozen solid and steel-like; it was almost impossible to remove it enough to get at some equipment.

We fought with our tents and somehow or other managed to get first one and then another erected, until finally, after frequent stops to get our breath back, we had five of them habitable. Pegs were useless in the snow, which, despite the absolute freeze-up of this terrible storm, had remained quite soft and could not support guy lines. We solved this one by driving in ice axes and our skis deep into the snow and attaching the guys to them. Gerry and I shared a tent and connected our tent lines onto the microlight. If the tent was blown away the microlight would hold it. If the microlight was blown away—well we didn't want to think about that too much.

We slept fitfully. Morning came, frozen and bleak, but the wind had subsided a little. The cloud rose slightly and we could make out our position. We had, as we thought, inscribed a huge circle on the glacier. We packed up and attempted to go forward. Gerry checked the compass in the Snowcat—it had been affected by the radio and some of our electrical devices. As a navigational aid it was useless, so Gerry agreed to travel in front on the microlight using his own compass to keep the bearing. It was soon apparent that this too was hopeless. The temperature was about -15°C and made co-ordination and communication difficult, while the wind, now increasing in its violence was blowing the micro sideways. Twice Gerry lost all sight of the Snowcat and we had to call a halt. Tortuously we retraced our steps to the camp of the previous night, almost losing Gerry in the process. And in zero visibility amid a snow storm we once again manhandled our tents into position. We used the Snowcat as a windbreak and Gísli elected to sleep inside

Right, top left: **The Snowcat on the edge of one of the many precipices we had to negotiate in our attempt to cross the glacier and reach the Ice Caves.**

Right, top right:

'Pterodactyl,
graceful, prehistoric bird
of giants
glides silent through
silken skies.'
Leon Vander-Molen

Right, bottom left: **The delicate microlight couldn't be transported over the rough glacier and so skis were attached to enable it to take off on the tundra where our camp was based, and land on the snow high up on the glacier where we planned to meet.**

Right, bottom right: **The microlight on skis being used as a snow vehicle with its engine running but without its wings.**

it. The rest of us were in tents. We needed some warm food and Gísli heated up some sausages. Benoit, trying to open a tin of ham almost severed his finger and Jean-Luc, our doctor, took over the Snowcat as a medical station. At the time I had not realised the extent of Benoit's injury and I got rather heavy with Jean-Luc for almost soiling the recording machine and camera. Understandably tempers were on shorter fuses in these conditions, but, good friends that we were, Jean-Luc and I cooled down and all was well again. Benoit made no complaint about his finger nor did he allow it to interfere with his work during the expedition, although it was bad enough to require stitching by Jean-Luc.

Accidents happen all too easily in these temperatures. For instance, during the previous day and before the storm really struck I had gone off to get some water from a small lake formed in the glacier's surface. Mick roped me up and we set off on skis towards the edge. Five feet from the edge, the snow cover gave and I fell through. Luckily there was quite a lot of thick slush on the surface and I managed to throw myself backwards and spread my weight before falling right through. I was able to fill the containers and then Mick pulled me away so that I could stand on skis again. It could have been serious, but the precaution of fixing the rope paid off, and our excellent clothing saved me from soaking—but accidents happen and we learned to be careful.

With most of us settled down into the tents, I had time to think about our situation. We had been travelling blind and with an inoperative compass in appalling conditions and, I shuddered to think, amid crevasses, some more than 25 feet (8 m) across, which could have swallowed not only the whole Snowcat but our 'crocodile' as well. I fell asleep thinking 'Thank God we've stopped moving.'

Snowed In

When I awoke, at around five in the morning, Gerry was very cold. He had in all, been exposed on his trike for about eight hours the previous day. I found him an extra sleeping bag and gave him some hot tea. As the team settled down with one another it became the practice for each person to look after the one with whom he shared a tent. Mick would bring Jeb his early morning tea and the following morning the opposite occurred, and so on.

The temperature oscillated between above freezing to below freezing. The wind retained its force and direction. When the temperature rose slightly, the snow and ice became water and rain and was driven into our clothes by the gale. Our clothes were soaking and the wet seemed to penetrate everything, even a complete set of waterproofs over several layers of clothing. The tents, sometimes covered with snow and ice, needed constant clearing, and then soaked with rain in the higher temperature, became deeply frozen when the temperature dropped again. Our clothes became like suits of armour, tents were board-like and the ropes stiff as steel hawsers. Movement became very much restricted. But we had to keep warm and active and so we worked. We dug out tents and we tried to cook. And we began to think this was going to last a long time. If it did, we would have to set up the camp better than it was right now.

We set to work building. Allocating one tent as a kitchen, we dug the snow from underneath it to give us more depth to move. The tent was dome shaped and now we cut a perfect cylinder in the snow to a depth of about 5 feet (1.5 m). The entrance was positioned away from the wind and when cooking, this was the most comfortable place on the entire glacier. We cut square recesses into the side walls of our galley and managed to store most of our food and equipment in these cupboards of ice. At least it would keep fresh!

Our next project was to build a toilet. It was impossible to relieve oneself on the surface of the ice as the removal of any layer of clothing allowed the wind to inflict painful lashes and to cut through clothes with ease. We decided to dig a deep hole in the snow so that the user would be below wind level. The temperature had by now dropped severely and with the fierce wind blowing particles of snow everywhere, there was a combined chill effect of below -35°C — cold indeed. As we dug our hands became numb despite our two pairs of thick gloves, but we stuck at the task and our toilet was eventually 6 feet by 5 by 5 (2 x 1.5 x 1.5 m). Within two hours the storm had filled it in and it was virtually obliterated. To walk was now a tremendous effort and still the wind increased—the laws of gravity appeared to have changed and to get from place to place we had to lean forward almost 30 degrees into the wind to prevent falling backwards. The trike that had stood 5 feet (1.5 m) above ground soon disappeared under the drift and all that remained visible was the vertical post sticking up in the air.

'Hotels'

By early evening three of the tents had collapsed under the weight of snow and ice and were completely buried. We had placed the Snowcat wrongly and now it was too late to move it—the trailer was completely iced in and the ropes were thick steel rods. We could not see properly for the icy cold pellets propelled by the gale blasted our faces, and layers of ice and snow built up rapidly on our clothing. With just two remaining tents we had to do something, and so within the comparative comfort of the Snowcat we devised how to build some ice caves. Jeb started digging but in two hours he returned with frozen feet. Benoit, Jean Jacques and Gerry took over—one to dig, the second to hold a plastic bag which when filled, would be handed to the third who stood outside the intended cave and fashioned this into a protective wall around the entrance. In spite of the appalling conditions, morale was high. I took over some digging and continued with Gerry. Each little team vied with the others to produce the best habitation—ours was 'bed and breakfast'—rather a far cry from *'Hôtel Napoléon de Paris'* excavated by Gísli and Gudbrandur. Theirs was superb, spacious and with a magnificent porchway entrance. These caves were another world. Once below the glacier level, the sound of the storm raging above was silenced and everything was serene—it was impossible to believe that the wind was attacking savagely with its fierce and fearsome cutting edge.

But our peace was shortlived. Silence was punctuated by an intermittent drip - drip - drip. We studied the roof of our new home with caving lamps which were fitted to our foreheads. A few minutes later we located the source. It was the rough back edge. We assumed that the snow was too warm or that we had dug too deep, cursed our luck and ventured out again. The snow had suddenly turned to rain, the temperature had risen and everything was rapidly being soaked through. Everything that had not been put under shelter—sleeping bags, clothes, tents, even food boxes that could not go in the kitchen shelves, had filled with snow which the rain was turning to icy slush. We fought our way back into the Snowcat, where icicles were now dripping, opened the door and

Main photo: **On our journey across the glacier the Snowcat led with Jean-Luc being towed behind on skis and the ever-adaptable microlight, also on skis, now being used as a 'snow vehicle'. Conditions when we set out were favourable.**

Left to right: **Conditions slowly worsened until the camp was completely buried and we had to dig ourselves out.**

'Tumultous, bustling
  crushing wind
gnashing unmerciful jaws
  of fury.
Contemptuous gale force
  rush in anger
consuming, devouring
in a frenzied gush,
a deadly breeze in a white
  summer freeze,
felling portable shelters.
Blizzardy
blind invisibility
damaged escape facility
awaiting a change
a chance
a glimmer of survival.'
                Leon Vander-Molen

climbed into the relative warmth, where, huddled in small balls in their sleeping bags lay other members of the team awaiting the weather change. Mick suggested that we flatten the roof of our ice cave and then build a gutter around the floor where it met the walls. He thought that all ice caves leak and drip and this was the way to allow the drips to run down the walls. Gerry and I returned to our cave relieved that we had not been digging for four hours for nothing. Soon the roof was smooth.

We visited Gísli's 'Hotel Napoleon' which was bottle shaped like a bottle of Mateus Rosé on its side. But the stench that issued from it was not the grape—Gísli had decanted some unclean petrol into the ice 150 feet (50 m) from the camp and the petrol fumes had reached his cave. Gudbrandur, not amused at having dug for several hours in vain, gave up in disgust and returned to the Snowcat, being quite unable to tolerate the smell. Gísli said he would stay the night and we promptly renamed the cave 'Benzine Hotel.' Gerry and I each took a survival bag and a sleeping bag and disappeared into our warren. We took a shovel for safety's sake. Our cave was quite small—the entrance was 5 feet (1.5 m) deep and sloped back at a 45 degree angle opening out into a simple box shape which could comfortably accommodate two, and at a pinch, three. It was pitch black without our lights and I kept striking my head on the roof each time I moved. But Mick's theory was borne out and we were quite snug. Nevertheless, we cocooned ourselves in special plastic survival bags to keep off unwanted drips.

Gerry, man of sky and space, felt claustrophobic and slept with his head nearest to the entrance. I did likewise. With foam mats beneath our sleeping bags for insulation against cold and damp, we slept as in another world, warm, cosy and silent. Two or three hours later I awoke, and turning to Gerry discovered that his head had become a black plastic bag, which shook me until I realised he had turned completely around and now had his head well into the cave and the bag was covering his feet. The wind changed direction and started to blow snow into our entrance. It got smaller and smaller until, thankful for the shovel, Gerry arose and dug out as far as he could. I changed my sleeping position and we both slept again. After three hours, I reawoke. Unbelievably the shovel that Gerry had left standing up in the snow by our feet was completely covered. My feet were buried in snow, Gerry was nowhere to be seen. He had gone to the Snowcat. Everything in the cave was soaked. All my fibre-pile clothes were caked in ice. I watched from the comfort of my bag while the entrance to our once roomy abode reduced down to a thin horizontal gap about 1 m high. The cave began to fill up and I knew that if the hole got any smaller I should have to move out. The cave would have to be abandoned, but it had one further role to play. Conditions outside made toilet procedures quite impossible. The wind had doubled in fury. But in this cave was the plastic bag we had used when digging it out—and for me this solved an urgent problem. We renamed the cave 'The New Toilet.'

Extract from my diary: '. . . I fought my way to the Snowcat leaning heavily towards the wind and fell over twice before reaching the door. The wind, now cutting through my clothes rocked the great Snowcat. I opened the door and it was ripped from my hands and slammed open, I thought for a moment we would lose it. I glanced back at the camp and throught the blizzard it looked a sorry sight—the tents would not hold for long . . . I took shelter in the cabin and shuddered at the wind's screams . . .'

The last two tents would not hold for long. Once in the warmth of the 'cat, we greeted each other. All seemed to be OK and Jeb suggested food. He and I went out again into the kitchen where we found a large plastic packet containing spinach. That is what it said—but it did not look like spinach, it did not smell like spinach and it certainly did not taste like spinach. We thought it more like dried herbs done in tea. We mixed it with melted snow and because it looked far from appetising we checked the packet three times to make sure it was supposed to be spinach. As the kitchen itself was beginning to fill with snow we placed two large food barrels in the entrance. They were soon snowed in and helped to reduce drifting into the kitchen. Like moths to a flame, the team were drawn to the kitchen by the aroma of cooking, and the meal of meat, biscuits, cheese, dried fruit and nuts was greatly appreciated. The spinach was not.

For five days now we had been trapped on this glacier. Most of our equipment was under the snow. The Snowcat and trailer were almost buried. Collapsed tents were under the snow somewhere and the microlight was identifiable only by a small tube sticking out of the snow. Filming was almost impossible and when Bruno attempted it, two minutes of film resulted in three hours of trying to dry out his camera.

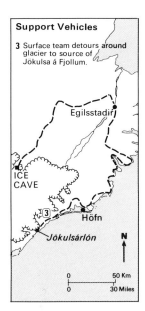

Race against time

And then Vatnajökull the mighty, relented. On the morning of the 8th August we saw the sun. The wind dropped and the snow lay powdery on the icy surface. We were to find out later that we had been caught on the glacier in the worst summer ever recorded in Iceland. Seven lows in the weather were crossing the whole country and we had just encountered two of them. This glacier is so large, it creates its own climate, which, when superimposed on to bad weather systems can lead to violent storms and raging gales.

The forecast, we heard, was of force twelve winds and extremely low temperatures. This was not the time to battle against such odds, and we should live to fight another day if we were now discreet and retired from the glacier (if we could). We thought we could make our way around to the ice caves at Kverkfjöll by the road which encircles Iceland. We had already lost much time and could not jeopardise the main objective of our expedition—the conquest of Jökulsá.

We packed everything in six hours, racing against the rapidly deteriorating weather. Digging out took almost four hours. The microlight was incredible. After removing it from its icy tomb, the engine started at the first pull. The only damage was to a pulley ring which had fallen off because of the temperature changes. The large trailer was firmly stuck in the snow and only by sheer brute strength could we pull it out. We snapped three of our largest ropes in the attempt. But there were one or two lighter moments when our spirits rose, and we laughed. One in particular stays in my mind.

While I was vacating my ice home, I had, as mentioned used a black plastic bag for a major natural function, thus christening the erstwhile home. The conditions up on Vatnajökull were absolutely appalling. Freezing cold, with everything rock solid and untouchable, there was little chance for the niceties of civilisation. However, the conditions did eventually ameliorate and the time came when the team started to dig out the camp, looking for buried 'treasure'. Imagine the turmoil—smashed down tents, holes in the ground filled with slush, lost tools, bags, boxes, ropes and so on—all awaiting the prospector with his shovel. One team member took it upon himself to dig

out the hole in which Gerry and I had been living and after some twenty minutes or so, with a whoop of success, announced to the world that he had found something. He displayed an intriguing black plastic bag and untying the knots at the top, thrust his hand inside to withdraw the prize. Imagine his face when he discovered what it was—our prospector was not at all impressed with his nugget of gold!

Encouraged by our first sight of the mountains around us, we started our descent and reached our first camp by 9 o'clock that evening. The wind was raging again and we watched fascinated as a waterfall, cascading down one of the protruding mountains, was literally blown back up again, before reaching the ground. The gale had turned the waterfall into a geyser. We rested and then carried on down the glacier tongue, slowly and with extreme caution, for the crevasses we had skirted on our ascent had become bigger and more dangerous and on several occasions we almost lost our trailers down these massive holes.

We eventually reached the end moraine at about 2 o'clock in the morning. We were weary but we had to keep going forward— time was no longer on our side. Abandoning the Snowcat near the lake, we transferred to our vehicles and, having decided that the only way to get the team and equipment to the ice caves at Kverkfjöll was for us to follow the road around the glacier, we set off for Höfn to reorganise some of the equipment, dry out and repair the tents, and generally sort ourselves out, before starting the journey. However, Gerry, not wanting to be totally beaten by the glacier, thought it would be possible for two of us to go straight across the glacier using the microlight. He estimated that he would need to climb to an altitude of 10,000 ft and then pass through a critical zone for 5-10 minutes and afterwards start the descent towards the Northern Edge. The plan was made. I would fly over the glacier with Gerry and the others could drive on the round road to meet us. Rendezvous was to be at the Kverkfjöll ice caves. The land vehicles would set off immediately while Gerry and I would wait a maximum of three days for good weather. The contingency plan if the weather didn't improve was for us to fly around the glacier following the coastal road. After the others departed in our two Olís-loaned land vehicles with all the equipment, Gerry and I spent the entire day of 11th August preparing for our flight. Vatnajökull had beaten us once—we would not be beaten again.

Flight over Vatnajökull

Gerry studied weather reports and I prepared survival equipment. We were excited at the thought that we were to attempt the first ever crossing of the Vatnajökull glacier by microlight. We took a compact first aid kit, a special radio beacon, survival food, a small cooker, two light-weight sleeping bags and a fold-up spade. (If we went down on the glacier and survived, we would build ice caves—we had learned from our recent experience that a spade could be more use than a tent.) We took one pair of skis with us and I wore ski boots. It would enable at least one of us to ski out if it were necessary.

My diary reminds me of what I was to wear on that journey. I recall that I felt like a penguin, so bundled up with clothing I could hardly move, but the question of clothing is as important as that of food. In extremes of temperature we wear layers upon layers, seeking to entrap warm air between them. My clothing for a one-hour flight over the glacier was a Damart sleeved vest with long underpants to my ankles. Over this, I wore a

Left, top:'Forward and below us was a small hole in the cloud and Gerry was diving straight for it. We dropped through ...'

Left, below: Having failed to fly over the glacier, Paul and Gerry were forced to follow the road around it, but the journey still was not easy. Strong winds kept pushing them away from their destination and they had to tack in order to get near it.

Left, below, right top: The crash! Huddling under the makeshift shelter made from the microlight wing. Thinking we would be most likely to crash on the glacier if we were to crash at all, we had packed a shovel instead of a tent.

Left, below right, bottom: Even the most difficult circumstances had to be recorded. Here Paul loads another roll of film into his camera whilst sheltering under the microlight wing.

single-piece fibre-pile suit, covered by a single-piece Thinsulate Ozee suit, coloured blue and orange, over which came an SP 27 jacket (an alloy-coated insulator) coloured dull orange and finally a two-piece seaman's overall in bright orange. Over my head, two balaclavas, one light and the other in fibre pile like fur. Glacier glasses as protection against snow blindness and flying particles, two or three pairs of gloves/mittens in fibre fur and crash hat completed the kit. For my feet, apart from several pairs of socks, I wore special three-part boots which could be used for skiing, climbing or walking. Gerry and I took the same size and could swap in an emergency. The temperature would have a chill factor of about -40°C, so cold that it could even penetrate through all these layers of specially-designed clothing.

Of our safety equipment, the beacon was about 5 or 6 cms in diameter and about 30 cms high. It would send out signals on the international civil distress frequency 121.5 or the military one 243. We also carried small personal location flares in a strip which could be set off by a charger hung around the neck, and a red, hand-held distress flare. Finally, I had a 'Mickey Mouse' compass strapped to my wrist—which more than proved its worth. Nothing was left to chance for even a short flight such as this, we prepared as though we would be away for days. We had acquired a healthy respect for the glacier and its weather system!

With everything loaded and ready by evening, we decided to do some last minute test flights. All was well and before retiring for the night we told the National Life Saving Association of our plan, informing them that we intended to take off at 6 am.

Morning came, we loaded the final items, set off for the take-off area and professed ourselves ready. The plan was to fly straight across Vatnajökull to Kverkfjöll, a distance of 52 miles (85 km) with an expected flight duration of 67 minutes. We climbed gently to 3000 feet over a small valley which had been carved out by one of the numerous glacier tongues falling from the glacier to the lowlands. We saw small lakes and a meandering stream, running through sands to the sea a few kilometres away. The visibility was excellent and the forecast good, with light winds only expected. As often happens there was a difference of wind speed and direction at various altitudes and Gerry had worked out his heading taking an average and attempting to maintain an altitude which would reflect this course compensation.

As we overflew the glacier edge we could see the extent of the crevassed area and realised that there was no landing place in an emergency. Fortunately, this 'critical state' did not last too long and as we gradually increased our altitude, to about 6000 feet, we could see how the mountains were enveloped in ice and snow. At this height, now above the glacier itself, the air was bitterly cold and with our wind speed of around 45 mph (70 km/hr) the combined chill factor was devastating. We had every reason to be glad of the precautions we had taken. We were heading in a north-easterly direction, approximately on heading 315 degrees and we could see the Kverkfjöll mountains in the distance.

After flying for some twenty five minutes we became increasingly aware of two problems which had manifested themselves a little earlier in the flight. One of these was the failure of our intercommunication radio system. There was so much interference it was quite impossible to talk to each other, even with the microphones pressed hard to our mouths. This special radio system which we had linked into our crash hats had been working well on test, and we could only conclude that there was considerable electric and radio activity in the area above the glacier. The second problem, and we thought it quite a serious one, was the reversal of Gerry's compass which was fixed to the microlight. For some reason, which we assumed to be due to magnetic influence coming from possible metallic deposits beneath the glacier, the needle showed 180 degrees (south) when it should have showed 0 degrees (north). My small compass on the wrist was unaffected but as we were at that time flying visually and could see our destination clearly, there was little need to use it.

In this flight we had reckoned that there would be a period when, in an emergency, we would have a good chance to glide back towards Höfn, and then there would be a portion of the journey as we approached our final area when, if in difficulties we could glide towards Kverkfjöll. However, in between these two potential safe areas there would be a flight of several minutes during which time, survival would be critical. We had, therefore, equipped ourselves to deal with some sort of forced landing on snow and ice on the surface of the glacier should we have a failure in flight. But at this time, with enough fuel for about one and a half hours and no apparent problems, our thoughts were far from questions of survival.

Relaxed and enjoying the flight, I began to take some photographs of the glacier and to orientate myself to include a picture of my skis, for the benefit of a sponsor. Jean-Luc had given me a Canon camera and when Gerry turned his head towards me suddenly, I was delighted and thought he wanted his portrait taken. I focused in on him and he turned his head away. He did it again, and then again and I thought he was fooling about. Then, remembering we could not talk on the intercom, I began to realise that perhaps something was wrong. It was. The engine's sound had changed in pitch and although I had at first thought it due to Gerry making adjustments to the mixture control and throttle, it soon became apparent that he had not. We were losing power and when I looked, the exhaust had literally broken off at its attachment to the engine. This design has security bolts which prevent it from falling into the propeller in the event of coming loose, and these were now the only things securing it. With as much as 30 per cent loss of power, we were descending. We needed to land. To our dismay, low cloud began to obliterate the glacier and soon it was no longer visible. Suddenly, we could not see Kverkfjöll ahead any more, and flying above the clouds we had no way of knowing where we would land or on what sort of terrain we would have to exist. Two things only were certain—we were losing height rapidly and soon we would enter the cloud itself—a dangerous and disorientating move.

Backtrack

Gerry made the decision to return towards Höfn. We had literally crossed the glacier to within a very short distance of the ice caves but couldn't risk going on. We had to turn back. We had been flying for about 45 minutes and had about 45 minutes of fuel left in the tank; we would just make it. We also had three small petrol containers strapped to the back seat in case of emergency, but I must admit we were not too keen to attempt to refuel *in flight*—the two pairs of mittens we were wearing would make handling difficult, and a slip might easily put one of the cans into the propeller.

Conditions deteriorated and soon we found it difficult to tell if we were sinking or the cloud was rising at the same rate. We had no way of telling if the cloud in fact descended right down on to the ground or if there might be an area below the cloud which would afford visibility for a forced landing. We could not risk any attempt to find out. We were both getting worried about our predicament. We felt trapped. Here we were in a wounded bird, losing control of our height and rapidly becoming blinded to our surroundings. We couldn't go up and we couldn't tell what the result of going down would be. Fatalistically, we just had to await a thud. We hoped it would be a soft landing . . . we hoped we wouldn't be injured . . . and we were realistic enough to know that we could be on a knife's edge. And again, we couldn't deliberately enter cloud—for once in cloud it is impossible to tell if one is upright or in a spin, or even upside down! We could, at this stage, just see Höfn, in the distance.

Clouds

Behind us, curling like an enormous surf wave, the cloud had risen and turned in on itself. It was well above us and coming fast towards us—to the left, and to the right—impenetrable white and grey. And below us—what lay there? Were we clear of mountains? Were we above a crevasse? We looked towards Höfn and to our dismay saw it disappear behind a cloud. We were now completely surrounded. Gerry removed his crash hat to scream at me—'Refuel!' Then he stopped me. And again—and again—three times he screamed and three times he cancelled the order. I pointed to my wrist compass and we set a bearing to where we thought Höfn might lie. We could not tell if we were yet past the glacier or still above it, but we were descending fast and estimated only a few minutes more before we dropped into the cloud. Gerry contemplated jettisoning all our survival gear in an attempt to obtain lift and thus prolong our descent, but he decided against it. Lower and lower we glided, our wheels now almost skimming the tops of the cotton wool clouds. Suddenly, I felt the microlight accelerate forward. He had pulled in the control bar and doubled our speed. Forward and below us was a small hole in the cloud and Gerry was diving straight for it. We dropped through and saw the glacier's edge and valley appear below us. The gap closed up immediately above us.

We were now under the cloud line and could see where we were going; we breathed a sigh of relief. My small compass had brought us back to our original route up the glacier and we were pointing towards Höfn. But we were very low on fuel, very low indeed and passing over a critical zone. We had been airborne for about eighty minutes and still had no sight of a landing space. With probably less than two minutes fuel left, we sighted a dirt track road between four electric pylons, and thanking all the powers that be, brought our damaged machine to land. The terrible Vatnajökull had dismissed us from her presence once more—we felt the blow keenly! Where we had landed, by great good fortune and to our surprise, was a group of French visitors to Iceland. They came to talk to us, offered us coffee, and were delighted that we could converse in their language.

One of them gave me a lift back to Gísli's house in Höfn, where his wife Soffie plied me with refreshments, and took me to get fuel. Gerry remained with his flying machine. When I returned, we refuelled the microlight, wired the exhaust back into place and flew into Höfn. A mechanic in a local garage welded the exhaust pipe into position and the various adjustment nuts and bolts were refitted and adjusted.

Reassessment

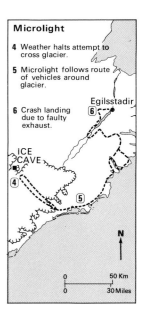

Microlight

4 Weather halts attempt to cross glacier.

5 Microlight follows route of vehicles around glacier.

6 Crash landing due to faulty exhaust.

Egilsstadir

ICE CAVE

N

0   50 Km

0   30 Miles

And so we had to consider our next move. There was at that time no question in our minds of going back over the glacier—it was just too unpredictable—twice bitten . . . but we had to meet up with the team in Kverkfjöll somehow and so we decided to fly around the glacier, using the road as a marker. There is a road which virtually encircles Iceland. It follows the coast and traces all the inlets and fjords, in and out of valleys and ridges. It is a very long and very circuitous route, but it would guide us as far as Eskifjördur where we would turn inland for a while, and then finally turn almost due south to arrive at Kverkfjöll (by following this route we would be making a rather wide circle of the eastern side of the glacier and would end up well to the north of our destination). It was indeed a very long way round but we thought it would be the safest bet.

The scenery was superb; valleys and ridges, farms and inlets, fjords and beaches. I was able to wave at people in the fields and farm houses. We had become quite well known in Iceland by this time and the media tried to follow our every move (although we didn't see them on the glacier!) But of course most people would have seen the press releases and were excited to see the microlight, looking for all the world like a three-wheeled motorbike with a kite on top. I took control for some of the time and Gerry studied maps. And so we flew pleasantly and steadily, in fine weather, admiring our view and relaxing. We would need to refuel after some while and Gerry was looking for a suitable landing area near to civilisation. We chose a small town called Djúpivogur and landed on a road. We found a petrol station and refuelled, then rolled the microlight down to the car park of the one hotel in town. We went inside to eat and hundreds of kids came rushing out from everywhere to look at the machine. When we came out, we felt like intrepid fliers from the days of Wilbur and Orville Wright. When we had assuaged their curiosity, we rolled the machine on to the road and got ready for take-off. There was not much space to manoeuvre. On our left was a large building, on our right, three lamp posts, and in front of us the harbour. We got away with little to spare and banked steeply to avoid decapitating the hotel—after their kindness to us it would have been churlish to land in the reception area, And in fact it was as well that we had done nothing to upset these kind people, for within about twelve minutes of flying, the welds on the exhaust had given way, and it was unrealistic to go further. We returned to the town and worked frantically to get it sorted out. By three in the morning it was fixed, but we were absolutely exhausted, so we slept, in beds, in the hotel.

On the morning of the 13th August, a significant date, we awoke, frustrated at our delays, knowing we should be in Kverkfjöll already, and fuming at the cloud which by now had covered the sky. We gazed around the village and its harbour. It would have looked picturesque, even romantic, if we had been able to see it all clearly, but the cloud was all around. Midmorning, a slight breeze arose and the cloud seemed to move and by lunchtime it was clear enough for us to fly. We had puffin and wine for lunch at the hotel, phoned Soffie at Höfn for a weather report, which was good and took to the air again. This time we made rather better progress. It was interesting to see how each of us viewed what we saw from the point of our own particular speciality—Gerry was entranced at the ridges, imagining himself gliding from them, while I was fascinated with the fjords and water courses, dreaming of myself in a kayak on their cool crystal waves. To economise on fuel and time, Gerry made some short cuts across inlets, always making sure we would be able to pick up the road again, for our experience on the glacier had alerted us to the rapid change of cloud position, which could arise. We made one or two landings for 'bolt-tightening' and to check on our miscreant exhaust, which did not look all that reliable. And on one occasion we were able to beg some more fuel from a passing car—the driver would have a tale to relate to his children when he got home!

While we were down on the ground, changing a bolt, we heard a high pitched whirring sound above us, and into view came the only privately owned helicopter in Iceland. I thought that perhaps the rescue services were looking for us but it was purely coincidence. After touch-down, we had coffee and the pilot talked to Gerry about the incredible wind variations in these rugged areas.

The Wind

We set off again and climbed high to get a clear overall picture of our route. Then descending we entered one particular valley which was closed off in a circular bowl at one end. There was some low cloud about and Gerry avoided it, slowly reaching the end of the valley. Some twenty minutes later we realised that we had not moved in relation to the ground. The wind had been directly head on and quite strong enough to negate our own forward impulse. We banked and flew cross wind to an adjacent valley, seeking less opposition. (If the wind had been at our tails we would have reached Kverkfjöll in half an hour). But this next valley, running from east to west, was extremely turbulent and once again we found the wind too strong for us and made no headway. Progress became impossible and we banked off away and landed on the dirt track road at the entrance to the vale. We had with us a small petrol cooker, so we had what all Englishmen rely on in times of stress, a good cup of tea. Some local people, curious, came to have a look and helped us to refuel.

We again took off, trying to cross the mountains and returned once more, soaked with rain, cold and dispirited. We discussed what our friend the helicopter pilot had told us. 'The wind here is against Kverkfjöll, but in the next valley it blows in the right direction.' We should have been able to use the lift created by the wind blowing against the valley wall. With enough height we could cross to this next valley and then should be in a position to start our final attempt to reach Kverkfjöll.

It was still raining and cold when we decided to attempt this cross over. The time was then 20.30 and we anticipated at least two more hours of daylight. We took off and flew along the valley which had repelled us before, searching for a suitable place to cross to the next valley. We tried to climb but there seemed no great feel of lift. We had hoped for some help from the wind on the valley wall but it did not materialise and if anything, we thought we were losing height.

Disaster

Then Gerry saw a place where we might cross and we banked over sharply, no longer flying parallel to the wall but straight at it. With just sufficient height to clear the top, we thought we were through when suddenly the bar was ripped from Gerry's grasp and the entire machine rolled violently over to one side. I was terrified! He regained control and tried again to penetrate the turbulence and cross the wall. We were flipped up at about 90 degrees and each time we were getting closer to the wall of the valley. We were being hammered back and forth with extreme violence and I thought we would be turned over completely. For four or five minutes that lasted an eternity, we were at the mercy of this wild valley and then, quite suddenly, all was perfect calm and we shot over the edge of the wall, into the quiet light airs of the plateau.

We both breathed a silent prayer and thought that we could now start to cover some miles, so while Gerry studied the map, I took the control bar. We had been flying for an age and I thought I ought to take advantage of this respite to check the fuel tank, so I turned around to feel the rubbery type container—horror and incredulity—it was empty—absolutely empty! I grabbed Gerry's arm and positioned it so he could feel the tank. We were flying on the fuel in the carburettor—and there was not much of that. Gerry took control again. Above the lake, and banking to improve our flying position we encountered a cross wind almost as strong as the head wind had been and we crabbed badly in the air. We found ourselves above another small lake, at about 200 feet height. The engine coughed, spluttered and stopped. Alarmed, I looked down. Below me and to the left and right I saw only water. Directly ahead was a steep mountain wall, with a patch of snow to the left. We started sinking like a stone and Gerry yanked the bar in fiercely to give us maximum speed so that we could try to manoeuvre. The ground rushed towards us and we hit the steep wall 100 feet (30m) from the lake's side. The microlight bounced up the steep incline and pounded itself into a patch of softer earth a little further on. The only sounds were the whistling wind and our sharp intake of breath!

'Are you OK mate?' asked Gerry.

'Yeah—fine,' I said without much conviction. 'How about you?'

'Dunno—my ankle hurts a bit.'

'We'd better see what's happened to the machine.'

We struggled out gingerly, taking care not to disturb anything—we couldn't tell at that point just how safe it was to move. Gerry had difficulty in putting weight on his foot and we thought the ankle had been crushed in the landing—we couldn't see if it was broken but it appeared to be in proper alignment and he could move his toes, so we thought it was probably all in one piece.

The undercarriage had been crumpled and we thought it would be a total loss, while the carrying rack was twisted at a right angle to its normal position. Gerry sat on a rock nearby. 'How in heaven's name did we manage to miss that?' We looked at each other. We didn't say so, but I knew that we were both thinking 'lucky to be alive for the second time in three days.' We did not say a word. I looked around. We were miles from anywhere. There was a lake, steep mountainous walls, patches of ice and all we had was a wing and a squashed trike. We dismantled and removed the wing carefully—it was to be our shelter for the night. (We remembered our decision to bring a spade instead of a tent, a decision taken in the expectation that if we had a disaster it was most likely to be over ice and snow. It was ironic that in this instance we had crashed on ground too hard for digging, and where a tent would have been the perfect shelter. Such are the vagaries of Icelandic fate.)

We pointed the wing into the wind, propped it up with a spare petrol tank, and Gerry, who was in pain, climbed into a sleeping bag and eased himself under the shelter. I brewed up, thankful for the survival equipment, and finding myself running out of steam, huddled up in my bag and slithered in next to Gerry. We were soon asleep.

Once in the night we were woken by a change in the wind direction and had to shift our makeshift tent, but soon went back to sleep again. We were warm enough under our cover, but outside, the wind blew, the drizzle fell and cloud enveloped the valley—and we knew not where we were. Nor for the time being, did we care, for we were totally exhausted.

Running Repairs

But, rested and alive, our natural resilience took over, and in the morning we had a closer look at our poor machine. We fashioned some tools and grips from our various knives and bits of equipment, and set to work dismantling the entire carrying system and the front undercarriage. If there was any way in which she could fly, Gerry would go alone and I would climb my way down, although at that time we did not know how high we were. It took us some time to pull the trike to bits, but when we had done so, we bent some tubing and twisted and hammered other parts, and cannibalised and made do, until some hours later we had the front wheel turning freely and Gerry thought it would survive one take off and one landing. It was no show piece but we were in no position to aim for perfection. We then put everything back, tightening as we went, adjusting tensions and as far as we could, ensuring her airworthiness step by step.

We refuelled—and she leaked like a sieve. We lost a lot of fuel and had to quickly empty the fuel tank back into the container. But when we looked for the leak we couldn't find it, and then realised that the fuel had been overflowing into the compartment below the tank. Next we discovered the exhaust had broken yet again and Gerry thought that this accounted for the rapid use of fuel above the valley which had caused our crash.

Lost

While we ate some hot food, and stoked ourselves up with nuts, chocolate and dried fruit for energy, we studied the map and tried to work out what lake we had crashed by. Now cloud closed in and soon we couldn't see the opposite bank, just 600 feet (200m) away. We had no way of knowing where we were—and of course, with Gerry's damaged ankle we couldn't walk out.

The wind increased and we had to anchor the wing down to keep our shelter in position. We could not have found a more inaccessible place and it began to dawn on us that we were not in a good situation. No one knew where we were. We did not know where we were. The team would by now be in Kverkfjöll, and as we had not been in touch with them for three days, they would be worried. Gerry's foot was badly swollen and I doubted if he could fly. He certainly didn't look as though he could walk. We spent the day wrestling with the problem of our location and three times changed our minds about our position.

Night fell and we saw some lights in the distance on a mountain far away from the opposite side of the valley, perhaps 40 km away. Car lights we thought, which would

Right: **Mick reaches the bottom safely and reaches for the second kayak. The smooth surface of the cave is caused by steam from the 'hot river' melting the ice.**

82   mean a road. Our maps showed that the only road which would correspond to the compass bearing we had taken on the lights, in fact placed our position on a completely different lake, far away from where we had thought we were.

Once again, the cloud descended and we climbed into our accommodation for a second night feeling not all that happy about our predicament. Gerry thought we ought to set off the special 121.5 emergency beacon, but I really didn't feel that we had come to that yet. I had no wish for the entire world to be out searching for us just because we had crash landed in the mountains. Had one of us been badly injured it would have been different—but we were both strong, and although worried, surprisingly unafraid. We did not use the beacon, and in retrospect I am glad. However, we tried out our VHF radio but its useful range was but a few miles, even when we used an aerial purloined from the plane and climbed to the top of the ridge above the lake.

In the morning, with cloud heavily surrounding us, it was not worth getting up so we rested until it had lightened. At about 9.30 we dressed and went to explore the surroundings to see if anything remotely resembling a take-off area could be found, and to try once again to fix our position. At the top of the ridge above our 'camp' was a slightly flattened area, with a good slope. We struggled to push the microlight up the slope to our new "aerodrome" but hampered by Gerry's painful foot and our rather exhausted condition, we found it very difficult. Gerry, forever resourceful, started the engine and the propeller helped us, but we had to stop every few hundred feet to rest. It was very heavy going.

But eventually, all the equipment and the trike were up at the top, and we were preparing to launch, when the wind started gusting. Quite suddenly conditions became impossible for take-off and we shrugged our shoulders and bundled in under the wing of the microlight for a third night and slept a dreamless sleep.

Trekking

We woke to an even fiercer wind and made the decision that we must try to walk out. There was pressure mounting on us to let the others know we were safe. We packed a minimum of equipment on our backs and set off due east—we thought that way sooner or later we would hit a road, or a farm if we were lucky.

We traversed streams, muddy swampland, small hills of rather sponge-like plants, and scrubland with small rocks. Two or three hours later we stopped near a moderate sized river. We refreshed ourselves and found some rocks which afforded a crossing. We were already soaked but Gerry thought that the cold water soothed his ankle, so he walked along in the river for some way. He made little complaint although he must have been in quite a lot of pain. To the side of the river was a ridge and we climbed over it. We were not really surprised to find that beyond this ridge was more wasteland and another ridge. But perseverance was rewarded—an hour later, and two ridges further on, we saw in the distance far below us, a small farm.

It took us a long time to get down to the land and approach the farmer. He spoke no English and what is more, did not understand our mimed explanations. We made aeroplane noises and showed with our hands how our plane had crashed. We were tired and we thought he was getting exasperated, so we pointed up to the mountains where we had come from and tried to indicate what had happened to us. He shook his head in disbelief that we had climbed and slithered down over 2000 feet (600m) of combined ridges, (and Gerry with his damaged leg). He welcomed us inside and we telephoned the Life Saving Association who, we discovered, were in the final stages of putting out a full scale search for us. We were to learn that our road-based team had had their own share of problems—but at least we were safe and they were safe. And Hannes Hafstein, Director of the Life Saving Association, was relieved—he did not have to give bad news to my parents who were on their way to Iceland for a holiday.

Overleaf, main picture: **Gudbrandur abseils down into the Kverkfjöll Ice Caves.**

Inset: **Bruno Cusa films and Jean Jacques records as Benoit and Jeb lower the kayak into the ice hole to reach the caves, while Mick abseils down. Mick had to abseil up and down** *six* **times for the benefit of the film crew, and stay stationary for five minutes; the ice screws had to be changed every half hour. Gudbrandur watches intently on the right, awaiting his turn.**

The Ice Caves

We learned over the next few hours that one of the team vehicles had broken down and was stuck in Kverkfjöll, while the other had a smashed suspension. Four days ago they had seen us when we were preparing to cross the glacier, and since then, nothing. Later Mick told me that once the weather had cleared up and we had still failed to arrive he had concluded we had crashed. We had some problems to resolve—our only microlight was stuck somewhere in the mountains and we did not know exactly where. Gerry had a bad ankle, some team vehicles were out of service and half the team was stranded in Kverkfjöll—problems indeed. We moved to a hotel in a small town nearby.

Gerry managed to hitch a ride from the helicopter pilot who was staying in our hotel, but first he was taken to hospital for an X-ray as his leg had swollen up badly and was giving him considerable pain. It was not broken, the report said. Cheered by the news Gerry and the pilot went to search for the microlight and, as the weather had cleared, launched it from the position in which we had originally placed it and flew it safely down the mountain to rejoin me. Newspaper reporters converged as he landed and asked us many questions.

We were very lucky to find a truck, an old four-wheel-drive war vehicle which we hired indefinitely and after some five hours of repairing the microlight, rewelding and cannibalising, we loaded it and all our gear into the truck and set off to rejoin our friends at Kverkfjöll. The road consisted of sand tracks marked every few kilometres with small white posts. We were able to negotiate steep inclines only because the sand was damp and thus more solid. The lava fields, torturing the tyres and hitting our weary backs, made the going very slow and we had to zig-zag about to find routes through. This vast area of red and brown tinted rock appeared to have come from nowhere, for we could not see a volcano. In some prehistoric age a fissure may have opened up and spewed its molten contents over the wastelands.

We drove for hours, and then in the distance we saw Kverkfjöll . . . the meeting with our friends was something I shall never forget. It was like meeting someone at a railway station you have not seen for years; you both want to smile but are too far away to talk, so you just walk slowly towards each other. They had been putting into action a retrieval plan because they thought we were dead. Mick had been rehearsing what he would say to my parents. Jean-Luc hit me hard on the shoulder—as hard as he could—to let out his worry 'Where have you been, you bastards? You've worried the hell out of us!' Around a wooden table in a hut built by an Icelandic explorer some years before, we recounted our adventures during the last five days. I had no idea at the time that Jean-Jacques was recording every word.

We were then brought up to date with their adventures since leaving Höfn on the road to Kverkfjöll—and here Mick takes up the story.

* * *

The Drive

'The drive from Höfn to Kverkfjöll on a sunny day is probably one of the most beautiful journeys in Iceland, taking in views of sea, lakes, cliffs, mountains, colourful valleys, glaciers, lava fields and deserts. This is just as well since the trip lasted almost twenty-one hours, and was not without incident in the way of punctures and breakdowns.

'Every now and then a river followed the road and sooner or later we would have to cross it. There were no bridges so the equipment had to be driven through the river. One of the team (usually me) would have to walk across the river to check its depth whilst the vehicles followed behind. I was persuaded on a number of occasions to take off my shoes and socks and wade in to find the shallowest crossing. This is not the most comfortable of occupations and after some considerable time at this, I got rather fed up with it, and suggested that as Gudbrandur was the driver and was supposed to know the terrain, he ought to take off *his* shoes and socks and paddle these icy streams. Gudbrandur flatly refused and something of an impasse occurred, until one member of the team came up with the bright suggestion that there should be a vote on it. A vote was duly taken, and by a narrow majority, it was decided that Gudbrandur *should* be the one to test the water. Accepting defeat with a good grace, he swung down from the vehicle, and duly took off his shoes and socks. But he didn't go straight into the water. No—he produced keys to a locker in the rear of the truck, and pulled out a pair of thigh length waders, which he proceeded to don! I had to laugh—we all did!

'We had made arrangements for a light aircraft to bring in to Kverkfjöll some stores such as fresh fruit, milk etc. There were no landing strips at the agreed meeting place, so after some rest, we set to work building an airstrip. We needed to clear some 2000 feet (600 m) of all stones and boulders, and indeed to find such a length of flat level ground, before the plane could fly in from Reykjavík some 250 miles (400 km) away. This highlighted the difference between the use of a plane and a microlight. We could land our lightweight pack-away microlight almost anywhere, on a road or a small 150 foot (50 m) smoothed area, which made it much more adaptable than a conventional plane. However, the payload which would be carried by the plane we were expecting would far exceed that to be accepted by a microlight and the distance in one flight would exceed its capacity. These are interesting comparisons and demonstrate the need to have a very flexible approach to the logistics of an expedition. The plane duly arrived and once landed, was unable to take-off through the rapidly deteriorating weather. We were forced to rope the aircraft to a small wooden hut during the night to prevent it from blowing away in the gale and in the morning "Kverkfjöll International Airport" (as Jeb liked to call our home-made airstrip,) was covered by a thick layer of snow. We reflected that if we had been using a microlight, it would have been dismantled and packed away until the weather improved—we could not pack away an aeroplane!'

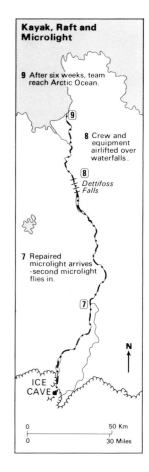

Kayak, Raft and Microlight

9 After six weeks, team reach Arctic Ocean.

8 Crew and equipment airlifted over waterfalls.

Dettifoss Falls

7 Repaired microlight arrives -second microlight flies in.

N

ICE CAVE

| 0 | 50 Km |
| 0 | 30 Miles |

The War of Hot and Cold

'Just a mile from where we were camped at Kverkfjöll, is one of the largest natural hot springs in the world. It cannot be seen even when one is standing just a few hundred feet away. The reason is quite simple—the glacier, on its never ending journey down to the lowlands, has blanketed the entire area with its icy coating. This is phase one of a continuous war between two of nature's most powerful forces—the hot springs, desperately attempting not to be cooled, attack the glacier by cutting snaking passages and convoluting chasms in its belly, while the glacier, mighty in its anger, sends blizzard after blizzard down on to the steamy vapour rising from within the ground. The vapours respond by cutting huge holes in the ice, holes which open the subterranean caverns to the sky. This fight has been continuing without quarter given or received for a thousand ages and is eternal. During the very cold arctic-like winters the glacier is supreme and the caves are threatened by snow and ice, but the arrival of summer brings relief from blizzard and as temperatures rise, the hot springs renew the attack, recutting the icy channels, regouging old vents and forming new ones.'

The Ice Hole

'We arrived at the northern edge of Vatnajökull, exhausted but excited about the next day's activity. After six hours sleep we awoke, to a cold blustery wind, promising bad weather and reminding us all of the power of the glacier. Paul and Gerry had not arrived and, believing them to be grounded by the weather, I asked Gudbrandur to monitor any weather reports he could, so as to estimate when they might arrive. The date was August 13th, an ill-omened day. We were already behind schedule, so I decided we would have to begin the attempt to get to the river at its highest point, which we had previously found out, was reached by descending through the ice. At the same time we had checked the exits. Paul and Gerry would have to join us there, whenever they arrived.

'Slowly, the team began to climb the glacier, returning at stages to pick up and carry canoes, climbing gear, filming and sound recording equipment, from the vehicles which were then parked close to the river. Some four hours later, we and our 'baggage train' were at the hole into which we were to descend.

'It was spectacular. Two rivers, one on the surface of the glacier, the other flowing from within, paired impressive waterfalls into a 100 foot (30 m) circular hole. These, together with crevasses on three sides, and a steep descent below gave the impression of beauty and danger together. I had worked out a safety system long before reaching this place, assuming (as it happened, quite correctly) that there would be no natural 'anchor points' for an abseil, and began the long careful task of rigging the ropes.

'Gísli had told me of the nature of the glacier's ice which was not really

Left, above: **A view to the steaming exit of the caves.**

Left, below: **Mick leads Benoit and Jeb out of the caves on the start of the long trip to the sea.**

'cold'. This meant that instead of the ice freezing solidly around the hollow tubular ice screws, it would slowly melt, leaving the rope supported by nothing but a hole full of water. I therefore, had to consider the work of not only getting the equipment and people down through this great aperture, but the need to change every screw at twenty minute intervals. I placed the first screw on the ice and began to hammer it. It is necessary to do this to give it some purchase before screwing it in. But instead of the usual 'ting-ting' sound which I had expected, I heard a dull thud—the ice was not good. Not only was it soft and warm, but it was rich in debris. Nevertheless, it would have to do. Traditionally a climber tests his own systems, so smiling, not only to give confidence to the others, but to hide my own slight fears, I launched into the hole backwards, away from the real world, into a wonderland of blue ice and water. Trepidation became exhilaration as I glided down the rope, passing through ages of time, the ice becoming more ancient each metre of my descent, my surroundings impressive and awe inspiring.

'Steam, rising from the river which gushed past my feet, and pushing my emotions into overdrive, heralded my arrival at the foot of the ice hole and I glanced upwards past the smoothed walls towards the sky, lighting the tiny hole that moments before had appeared so large. I made my way slowly along the river bank, the lamp I held revealing more of the riches of nature with every step I took and saw thousands of tons of ice over my head and on each side of me. The entrance of this cave was flanked with icefalls, which brought me to the realisation of danger—and I decided to return to the others.

'An hour later the descent proper began, lowering canoes, equipment and men into the hole. Jeb and Jean-Luc helped with safety, holding security lines and sorting ropes, whilst I directed the operation. It took three hours for us to arrive as a team, where we stood at the waters edge, looking upwards at the tiny sky hole—exhausted but very satisfied.'

A Bath Under a Glacier

'We were now all in the caves and we set up a small tent to protect our fragile camera equipment. The Jökulsá river is formed from the melted ice of the Vatnajökull glacier. Glacier rivers are icy cold and it is this which provides one of the greatest problems for the kayakist.

'But here, unbelievably, the water was not only unfrozen—it was warm—warm as a bath. Jeb yelling 'This is more like it!' stripped off and immersed himself in the first bath he had had for weeks. The rest of us were not slow in copying him—it was sheer unabashed luxury, and I think we might have stayed there for a long time—but we had an expedition to get on its way, and reluctantly we got into our canoeing gear and went to explore the exit of the caves, still wondering at the paradox of a huge, forbidding glacier of almost impenetrable ice, forming the roof and walls of a heated cavern with running warm water . . .'

'On the afternoon of August 14th 1983, we started the first ever exploration by kayak of this under-ice source. In places the river was only just deep enough to float, and we scraped against rocks. The actual exit was small reminding us of the London Underground tunnels, only here there were no tracks or trains, but a river and three canoes—Benoit close behind me and a little way behind him, Jeb, the rafter from Colorado, demonstrating his versatility as a kayakist. Within twenty minutes we had reached the exit of the cave. The four Frenchmen followed on foot with the equipment, assisted by the Icelanders.

'Outside again, we explored the nearest portions of the river, hoping to press on. But the weather was still bad and it was unsafe to proceed without scouting. This we could not do without a microlight, since the thick lava banks and surrounds of the river made movement almost impossible.

'And the weather continued to deteriorate. The team was worried about Paul and Gerry but I tried to reassure myself that they were OK. The thick snow which had covered the ground on our third day on this river must have prevented them from taking off. But they were very overdue! We carried on slowly, filming and exploring—then, on the morning of the fifth day, the weather changed dramatically and we were blessed with a Mediterranean type sun. We were sure that we should very soon see Gerry and Paul fly over the river, but by late morning, we were all seriously worried and, calling the team together, I told them that we would go to Grímstadir, some four hours' drive away, to find Paul and Gerry. Leaving the others to deal with the equipment, Jeb, Bruno and I travelled as fast as we could overland to Grímstadir. We took the Econoline van, leaving the other vehicle with Gísli. My thoughts were gloomy—what would I tell Paul's parents who were on their way to join us? Supposing both my friends were dead? I thought of how to get a plane to bring their bodies back home . . . such awful thoughts! By 8pm we arrived at Grímstadir to the news that they were alive and safe. There are no words to describe our feelings—but I know that for the first time in five days, that night I slept soundly.

'The following day we met them in a hut in Kverkfjöll and told our stories. Paul now resumes the story of Iceland Breakthrough.'

* * *

Gerry and I, hearing this vivid description, climbed our way into the caves to see for ourselves this paradox of nature. We took with us a special light used by Bruno for filming and made our way down the ice tunnels. Well up into the cave there were two channels of water, one hot, the other cold. We laughed and wondered if anyone would like to live in a place where there was already hot and cold running water laid on. Should we put up a 'bed and breakfast' sign? We made our way to where these two streams met, and found just the place where the temperature was bath-like. We refreshed ourselves swimming amid the blue/white ice, and watched the steam rise up to the walls,

92 smoothing them to a glistening sheen, almost silvery in reflected light. Feeling perhaps that all our trials were behind us, and that our perseverance had been rewarded by this luxurious interlude, we returned to camp and joined the others for the main kayak descent of our river—Jökulsá á Fjöllom.

The Jökulsá Descent

The River, in Detail

To understand what we were attempting we need to have a close look at two things. We need firstly to know the shape and condition of the river, its quiets, its rapids, its falls, dangers and passages. And we need secondly, to think about the whole conception of using the microlight in conjunction with kayaks and rafts in this field of endeavour. So, firstly, I will briefly outline the course of the river as it flows from the ice caves from which we had newly emerged. The river proceeds, complex and braided, and split into many channels, but in the main flowing slowly, and with little white water at first. At some distance from Kverkfjöll, it is joined by another river called Kreppa, itself substantial in flow, which transforms the Jökulsá into a much larger and faster run. It continues to increase speed and volume, and as the banks become narrower, minor rapids at first appear. Then more interwoven sections with sand or gravel banks, indicating shallows, gradually give way to speeding water, turbulent channels and increasingly wild rapids. This pattern continues for a considerable distance until the river reaches the canyon known as Jökulsárgljúfur, about 20 miles (30km) of beautiful rock formation and savage water. Here there are four major waterfalls, the first, Selfoss, horse-shoe shaped and catapulting its waters deep down. The water gathers itself together, and speeds around a 2500 foot (800m) curve to plunge headlong over Dettifoss, the mightiest waterfall in Europe. Plunging and rearing like stampeding horses, the water stallions tear at breakneck speed to find the north. Water, brown and thick with chocolate-like mud, churns foam into white and throws spray high into the air to glint with all the colours of the spectrum, into gorges and canyons, and then reaches Hafragilsfoss, to plummet into the depths. Then a few more kilometres down river the last of these four major falls receives the galloping herds and relays them on in a maelstrom of heaving manes of water and spray. It is called Réttafoss.

From here the river levels out and becomes faster and faster, raging through great rapids and twisting and turning, cutting into the rock and fighting to reach the sea. For many kilometres there is severe turbulence and unabated in its speed it scours a wider channel, which gradually opens out into a sandy plain. The river once again becomes braided and slows itself, until slightly further north, it bifurcates to enter the Arctic Ocean in two streams. In all it has travelled 128 miles (206 km) from source to sea and has shown its many moods in profusion. This then, is something of a picture of the river we were to explore by an entirely new technique.

The Concept

What is so special about the technique we had envisaged and were about to test out? If we had undertaken to kayak down the Jökulsá without using a microlight we would

have been forced to scout every section ahead on foot or by truck. In this terrain, with jagged lava fields and often almost impenetrable formations, we would have been slowed down to a snail's pace and the venture could have taken many months. In the completely impassable areas of the waterfalls we would have been forced into portering our canoes and equipment widely around the areas, very often on foot. There would have been considerable risks to the water craft, for it is not easy to scout on foot and dangers can be overlooked. The idea of using the air as a method of reconnaissance was attractive in that it gave the expedition greater flexibility and a higher safety factor when approaching hidden dangers.

The bonus of being able to transport men and equipment, including kayaks, over violent areas, was in itself a vital part of the concept. With our floats intact (recalling the 'Titanic' disaster on the lake), we would be able to overfly obstructions, carrying kayaks and gear, and alight either on the water or on the land as the occasion warranted. In actual fact, because of our various misfortunes, we were forced to make some changes, and during the descent of the river, our microlights kept wheels on. This did not in anyway detract from the project nor from the proof that the theory was exploitable and practical.

Lastly, microlights have two very great advantages over conventional aircraft. They can be very rapidly dismantled; it takes but twenty minutes to convert a flying machine into a set of units, packed in plastic and ready to be roped onto either a truck or in the river sequence, onto a raft, and secondly they do not need long runways. Provided the ground is free of serious obstructions, they need about 200 feet (60 m) for take-off and landing. They are light and can be manhandled quite easily in difficult terrain—but the most important feature, and one which made the whole concept so unique, was their complete adaptability from the air to the water or to use the emotive phrase, the aeronautical to the nautical and vice versa.

Starting Downstream

On August 21st, we were ready to start, albeit without the use of Gerry's microlight, which had suffered further damage to the trike and needed a day's work to get it in good enough condition for the rest of the expedition. Knowing that Simon Baker, our second micro pilot was due to arrive at any time, and realising also that some spare parts which we needed for Gerry's plane might be on their way, we decided to stow the damaged microlight on to the larger of our two rafts, and to proceed down-stream, expecting Simon to catch up with us. When we had packed it all down, the trike unit looked like a figurehead on the Avon raft and pointed the way ahead majestically. The propeller, lying horizontally, made the raft look like a waterborne helicopter.

'Hey—look over there!' someone yelled—and pointed to a speck in the sky, just over the distant mountains. The speck was the harbinger of good fortune, Simon Baker, carrying in his microlight the redoubtable Gísli, who had been back in Höfn with the Snowcat. They landed on the sandy bank and we all exchanged greetings. Simon then took to the air again, and again, each time carrying a team member with him as observer to scout the river ahead. Jeb, as one of these passengers, reported that the river looked

good except for a few minor rapids. Gerry at that time was fretting and fuming with impatience at being grounded—or rather 'water-fast'—for, truth to tell (as he later informed us) he was not that keen on shooting rapids on a raft—he was strictly an airman. We set off, Mick in the lead kayak, and were surprised when he signalled for us to pull over to the side. We had encountered one of the apparently minor rapids, which had proved, on closer inspection, to be not as minor as aerial observation had implied. We had to consider this effect of the scale of rapids as seen from high above, and were able later to determine some 'measuring' techniques to avoid under-estimation of dangers.

We all drew to the side of the river and clambered out on to the sharp columnar lava bank. A quick look at the river alerted us to the discrepancy between the appearance from the air and the reality of its fierce mêlée when viewed from the bank. We saw partly hidden rocks and the dangers of dirty muddy water which obscured sharps and jags in our proposed route. In a kayak the expert tries to follow a route which he has planned when inspecting the river—but it looks quite different from the seat of a pitching, twisting, heaving kayak, with water gushing into the face, and concentration razor edged into maintaining a survival position. With ease, the power of the river can drive the craft from its path and the kayakist then brings into play all his learned expertise and power, looking to regain his chosen route but, in the event fighting the river to keep control of his position, and above all to prevent a beam-on approach to rocks. The finest judgement of a kayakist resides in the knowledge of himself. He must have complete understanding and there must be no illusions about his ability to deal with situations. He must be brave enough and wise enough to refuse to enter battle with an overwhelming rapid. He and only he, will be able to make this judgement—and danger awaits the man who takes this lightly.

The entire perspective of the river changes from this low seat in its bosom. Like a fish, the kayak is controllable when it is either faster or slower than the stream of water. At the same speed, there is a sort of overdrive effect with consequent loss of control. The choice of route would be reached with avoidance of obvious dangers a prime consideration. Such obstacles as visible rocks, indications of submerged rocks, 'stoppers', whirlpools and a 'reversed curve' of current turning back on itself into an eddy would be observed and remembered. The route would have been discussed and agreed with companions before setting out and a signalling, security and rescue procedure would have been thoroughly established.

Speeding at 20-25 mph and making instinctive reactions to changes of the water, sudden unexpected forces can take the kayakist unaware, and it is here that survival may depend upon the skills practised in rolling and in perfecting the almost aerobatic acrobatics of the slim fibreglass craft which has become almost an extension of the controller's body. Rolling is an art form, where movement of the trunk at the same time as an underwater thrust with the blade will bring the kayak upright, with a minimum of delay. Kayakists in these very cold waters do not delay the roll, a feature of which is frequently a tight pain around the head, like the inquisitor's leather thong.

Imagine taking a seat in a thin streamlined container, a mere 3 mm thickness of fibreglass and setting sail upon a turbulent river. At once, and with frightening power, it is thrown upwards to 14 feet (4 m) above, twisted, bumped, pitched and tossed over the crest of a mighty wave, and then with a stomach-wrenching drop, cast down into the

drop, cast down into the unknown valley on the far side, to bury nose and rider into the rising curl of the next wave. If you are lucky, it is clean and green and you will glide up its slope and pitch over to the next valley. But if not—or if there is but the slightest mistiming, this same wave will obliterate the sky, and break down upon you with terrifying power, making you grasp the paddle with all your might and hang on for dear life to maintain a survival attitude until, if luck remains, the river has had its way with you and spits you forth from the maelstrom. The kayakist learns to read the river's signposts—the rocks and then the 'stoppers', those convolutions of water reminiscent of the twisting whirl of a front-loading washing machine, into whose hungry maw the unwary canoe may be sucked—and held down. There are hazards of fallen trees (though not much likelihood of this in Iceland), of turn-back eddies and of huge waves, cresting like seaside surf which kayakists call 'haystacks'.

Self awareness in these cold waters is important—not just the absolute knowledge of skills possessed and the tested familiarity and trust of carefully chosen equipment, but more. There is the understanding of the indications of change within the physique itself. When the kayakist first enters the river, there is the cold. It is within and without, and he must await the onset of the internal heat of exercise to give him the central heating he requires within the cold house of the river. The temperature of his hands indicates to him what his situation may be, acting rather like a thermostat and he will understand that his hands will be warm enough within about five minutes of his run, and that it will be some three hours (on average, for we are all different) before they start to cool. He should know that the cooling of the hands is the buzz of the thermostat telling him to switch off and rest.

In an expedition such as ours, the kayaks had many roles to play—they were probes and they were security for rafters who might go overboard, and for each other. They were supremely effective craft and our handling of them was enhanced by our confidence in each other and the economy of our communications.

The rafts demonstrate a rather different approach to the 'in-water' syndrome. They are flexible and bouncy. They will strike a rock (provided it is not a jagged one) and bounce off it. Their route is not necessarily the same one as that chosen by the kayaks, but it will be planned to avoid major problems like 'stoppers', large 'holes' in the water and particularly to avoid being drawn to the sides of the river and jammed against walls. There is the danger of capsize and the great amount of effort required to keep steerage way in severe turbulence will tax the strongest of oarsmen, this making fatigue a major hazard. But, handled with skill and with due respect for the power of water, they are the most versatile of vehicles and proved invaluable to Iceland Breakthrough.

We regained our seats and positions and then Jeb, in the large raft carrying Gerry, Robert and the stacked microlight, took the route right down the centre of the rapids, just avoiding some large curling back waves. Gísli followed in the second smaller raft, carrying Bruno and Jean-Jacques—all were safe. Mick, Benoit and I ran through in our kayaks and exhilarated by the challenge of this first rapid, returned to run it again as a warm-up exercise for the more violent ones which we knew would be challenging us later. Simon flew above us, like an eager seagull trailing a fishing fleet—small wonder Gerry was frustrated on the water. And meanwhile, our trusty friend Gudbrandur, was making his way down the bank of the river with the support vehicle to meet up with us some days later.

Right:

'River of Iceland
ignored
unexplored
we will cleave your
    currents raging,
guarding treasures
plunging, braiding,
    twisting
to allure us
can we leash your
    awesome power.'
Leon Vander-Molen

After we had safely come through these rapids, we continued downstream, where the river opened into many braided channels. The wind in Iceland is everpresent and arises when least expected. We now encountered a severe cross wind, which tended to blow the rafts over to the starboard bank of the river. The difficulty of manoeuvring the rafts against this wind, and seeking channels and passages in the complex water system, was taxing to the rafters and by the time we were approaching the next set of rapids, Jeb and Gísli were showing signs of exhaustion from constant rowing and fighting wind and water. We made the decision to call a halt, set up camp, regain our strength and save the attempt on the rapids for the morning. We had completed our first full day on the Jökulsá—and already we had sensed the promise of drama and danger ahead. We were not to be disappointed.

We awoke the following morning to clear blue skies, a sparkling sun and just a few small clouds. And to our joy, absolutely no wind. Because of the wind on the previous night we had dismantled Simon's machine and we now had to reassemble it. We set it up as quickly as we could and then Simon and I took off from a wide open sandy beach, by the river's edge. Rising above the camp, we circled and made our way towards the next rapids. The river in this section is divided into three separate flows, which just south of the rapids, come together in one mighty water explosion. Even from our altitude above the river, it was impressive to behold. We saw thick chocolate liquid heaving its way over the rocks and filling in every gap and gully in the walls of the gorge as it passed through, for all the world like a giant praline confection with its whips and whirls—could this be the seat of so much danger?

In five minutes I had seen all I needed to see. There was a clear route down the right-hand side of the river and no dangerous water formations to cause problems. I could also see well below the rapid for some 4 miles (6 km), and was pleased to view a relatively calm flat of water where we could effect a rescue if someone went into the water. We landed back, and then Simon took the other kayakists and rafters, one by one, to have a look at the scene. Suitably briefed, we checked lashings, tightened our girths so to speak and shot the rapids. From the bank, Bruno filmed and Robert took stills. Jean-Luc in the raft took his photographs and bailed while Simon oversaw the attempt from 200 feet up. The water which had looked quite thick and almost slow from the air, was violent and turbid, and we were pitched from side to side, thrown up and then down, turned around and twisted, sucked down and then spat out by the raging water—the oarsmen fighting desperately to maintain position in the flow, while their crew bailed, filmed and then bailed again. Water attacked us from every direction, stinging our hands and faces, soaking through where protection was lacking and mingling with the sweat of our exertions. But we came through and when we had reached quieter water, we looked around and breathed a sigh of relief that we had negotiated this difficult stretch without any more incident than Benoit having to perform some eskimo rolls, which he did with his customary *sang froid*. The excellent film footage we obtained was reward for the effort—and we had overcome another obstacle.

Dettifoss

We now take a small jump forward in time—we have moved on down the river, Gerry's machine has been put into working order and we are on the approaches to Dettifoss, that tremendous waterfall, standing as a barrier angled across the waters of Jökulsá á Fjöllum. We are in camp just 3 miles (5 km) from the entrance to the Jökulsá canyon. We had shown for the first time that microlights could be combined with kayaks to form a very powerful method of exploration. We had used floats as an undercarriage to takeoff from water and to scout the way onto the glacier. We had fitted the microlight with skis and had even used these to take off from grass. The microlight had proved its worth on the glacier, travelling as a new type of snow machine. We had saved days by using these packaway aircraft to scout terrain and rapids for us, and we had even carried one through rapids strapped to a raft. And now we were preparing for the final test—could the microlight carry members of the team and their craft from above, or even from within a deep canyon and transport them to the river section below?

In seeking to test out the use of the microlight as an 'aeronautical/nautical' agent, we had in mind the concept of a completely new appoach to exploration, which might be used by expeditions in the future. It was thus imperative for us to test our theories under extreme conditions. No purpose, from this point of view, would have been served if we had simply flown *around* the waterfalls. We would need to expose the machines with their pilots and cargo to the most testing circumstances we could find. Imagine if you will, a scene in which a giant natural obstacle, such as the Niagara Falls has been transplanted from its bedrock and placed across a gorge, in the Grand Canyon of the USA where the walls of this natural fissure are in some places *one mile high!* We can almost feel the spray, the turbulence, the sheer chaos. We can almost hear the crashing of millions of gallons of water. We can sense the shudder of rocks under the impact of tons of flying, lashing, heaving river strains. In such conditions, only the most expert fly—for who would dare to brave the downward suction of the plummeting water without enough manoeuvring space to bank away and climb? Who would risk the unexpected updraughts and downdraughts which occur as a result of temperature changes within the confines of the canyon walls? Who risk flying through the funnel effect of the wind which can whistle and whine through narrow gorges, its speed enhanced by the restriction of width, and its turbulence increasing with every obstacle which could divert it from its course? And who would risk the plane *one mile* deep down in the canyon, to fall between massive water obstructions behind and ahead and implacable walls at each side—to attempt to ascend the great height and then fly over—this could make the worst kind of prison for a flier . . . who indeed? And yet—and yet if we could solve the problem of air turbulence, there could be a way—it might *just* be possible for an expert flier to plot a course designed for the maximum avoidance of air disturbance. All conditions would need to be perfect, but maybe it could be done. Dettifoss would be our Niagara and to overfly this great waterfall was one of our principal aims. It would be the climax of our expedition, we thought, and would help us to point the way to the future.

To discover the capacity of our machines we would fly as low over the falls as the turbulence would allow; we could not even begin to estimate the effects of such turbulence on a microlight with two kayaks attached to it, and two men on board (or with a cargo of equivalent weight and mass). But these conditions would show us what might be achieved with planning, high expertise and the will to succeed. No pilot would attempt to take his aircraft into such conditions without very careful planning, and a very close study would have to be made of the air currents—how they rose and lowered,

Overleaf:

'Cascade of aggression
uncontrollable
with fiery talons of
passion and
possession,
like a dragon
astride the rocks.'
Leon Vander-Molen

The team, seen here as tiny specks, give a sense of scale to this awesome scene. They are checking out Dettifoss in an attempt to assess the effect of its turbulence on the microlight.

how they circled and became whirlpools to entrap the unwary. A course would have to be found to avoid draughts which would throw the microlight against the canyon walls. At what height would the pilot fly? And at what speed? There were many questions to be answered, and one of these was, what effect will *kayaks* have on the *airframe* stability of the micro when in severe turbulence? The largest question concerned the wind. Quite obviously a strong wind would be completely counterproductive, but how slow would the wind need to be before an attempt could be made? Or should we wait for no wind at all? We were about to try something never before attempted—to fly our frail craft over the greatest of nature's obstacles, where even the rules of atmosphere were subjected to the massive force of water spray, mist and turbulent air—we dared to challenge Dettifoss, where no person had dared before! With these thoughts in our minds, we awoke on the morning of the day before the attempt on Dettifoss was to be made, and as we made our way towards the waterfall, Gerry and Simon were deep in thought. They stood for hours, studying the turbulence of the microcosm created by the thousands of tons of water which hammered over the rocky edges.

'There is a problem,' Gerry stated. 'Because the falls are set at an angle of about 45 degrees to the river's flow, the wind tends to be thrown against the left bank. This creates a whirlpool of turbulence in the air on that side.'

Gerry and Simon planned their approach and decided that they would make for the right side of the river to avoid the danger area. The weather was suitable for flight, so they took to the air separately, and spent some hours experimenting with different altitudes, testing the turbulence close to the falls, sampling routes and establishing safety procedures. Various options in the event of an enforced landing were discussed and the action simulated as far as possible. There was a tacit agreement that in the event of a failure of the plane, the pilot would try to crash land as close to the right bank or wall as he could, for it was on this side of the canyon that the majority of the team would be stationed, with ropes, climbing gear and the impedimenta of rescue, as well as the photographic and recording equipment.

Mick, our climbing expert, studied a way down into the canyon base, and designed a rope system to enable a descent to be made if need be. He had made an enquiry in depth about the geology of the area during one of our early reconnaissance visits, and was well informed as to the correct tools to apply to the rock, the depth of its various ledges and crevices. We were confident that this side of our attempt would be completely under control. Radio communications would be of vital importance in this combined operation, and we set up a connection which would enable Simon (with Bruno as his passenger) to have two-way communication with me. I would be able to speak to and to hear the members of Mick's team from their station on a ledge down a canyon wall on the right and in addition, to have communication with Robert and Jean Jacques, who were to be placed, for filming, on another part of the canyon's wall.

The whole day passed in these preparations—the fliers experimenting, the climbers testing systems, the photographers checking angles and light, cleaning lenses and over it all, the crackle of the radio occasionally heard above the roar of the water. In the evening the wind rose slightly and warned us to return to camp, where we ate, slept and prayed for perfect weather, Microlights demand fair weather conditions with low winds. For tomorrow we needed perfect vision, no cloud, no wind, and a heavenly spring-like day.

Our prayers were answered—heaven sent us a spring-like day and we set to the work of strapping the kayaks to the special carrying racks we had built, while Gerry checked out the aircraft. The time approached for us to get to our respective stations. Simon took Jean-Luc over to the left cliff top from where he would take still photographs and, knowing that time was precious, we thought with some sense of achievement that this small ferrying operation which would normally have taken almost a whole day, took but a few minutes in our versatile microlight. Simon returned and picked up Bruno and his marvellous movie camera. Gerry was to be the first to make the attempt. The rest of us were to ensure that it was filmed and that he had maximum safety cover. We moved into place, Mick and his team down on a canyon ledge, somewhat further downstream from the falls, while Robert and Jean Jacques found themselves adaptable vantage points so that they could vary their shots as the bird flew down the canyon, while I positioned myself very high up on the canyon wall for the best radio reception and visual control of the operation. Once we were in place and all communications had been set up, I radioed to Bruno and Simon, who were still at camp with Gerry 'We're all in place here . . . over.'

'Roger. We are about to get airborne . . . over' came the reply.

And with this we launched into our first attempt to conquer one of nature's most formidable barriers. If this worked, we could go anywhere in the world with our system of kayaks, rafts and microlights. If it didn't . . . we tried not to think of that.

Flyover and Over

Bruno on my signal told Simon it was all systems go and with a sign to Gerry, they became airborne. Above the waterfall, my eagle's eye view was absolutely superb. Spray was thrown in all directions in the canyon below and the water seemed to glide over the edge in a slow mesmeric action, drawing me towards it. I had to look away and I saw the microlights appear in the distance like two birds planing through light airs. As they came closer I could just discern the two slim cylinders of the canoes attached to the frame of Gerry's machine. I knew that they were approaching at 40 mph but from my vantage point they appeared to be still. The scene was unreal—the noise of the waterfall, pounding rocks, roaring its mighty territorial cry, the warning of savage ownership, sending down into the depths thousands of terrifying tons of uncontrollable water, was all-pervading and overpowering. Speech was almost impossible, amid the spray, confusion and chaos, and above, serenely contrasting with nature's wild confusion, two winged creatures floated like Red Admiral butterflies, the blues, reds and whites of their wings reflected in the sky. Would these beautiful creatures be drawn towards the water by the awful power of the falls—like moths to the flame?

Gerry was now some way in front and I saw him shoot over the top of the fall, at a height of about 100 feet (30 m) above the surface. I glanced to the left and saw Simon following closely. Gerry had been carried slightly towards the left hand and was fighting in the turbulence he had sought to avoid. I saw, with increasing alarm, the control bar being wrenched almost out of his grasp—now to the left, then to the right, now turning clockwise and then anti-clockwise, rising, falling, banking, and twisting and tossing from side to side as the pendulum of some frenetic timepiece, and yet in these dramatic seconds, time stood still. I glanced at Simon's flying machine—they had drawn closer, as

Overleaf, left:

'Let your water fall
far out of my reach
I'm aflight
from your tongue-like
      grasp
such a painting of power—
with every brush stroke
feel an artist's pain
pleasure, lust and bliss.'
Leon Vander-Molen

Overleaf, right:

'Pterodactyl of elegance
butterfly of strength
sweeps through the air
an eye on the river.'
Leon Vander-Molen

close as they could dare, to film the battle raging in the spray laden air and I noticed, through my glasses, that Gerry, in the very heat of the moment, had still retained control enough to flick the switches of the two cameras attached to his own airframe—of such men was the team composed! Suddenly he was torn from my vision— wild fears assailed me—two seconds, five seconds, then ten, then twenty, forty—or was it a hundred years? I could not tell . . . it was an eternity of fear.

And amidst this sick fear, there arose in the distance, first the wing and then the trike of Gerry's machine, far down the canyon, and making towards me. He came closer and closer and zoomed down low as he reached my cliff top, to give his victory salute. He flew far away above the falls and then, to our delight and applause, made a second run—to prove that the first one had not been just a matter of luck! We gained many films and photographs of the scene and we revelled in the success of the attempt. It was good at last to feel that we could win through, after the defeats and setbacks of our early days on the glacier. We celebrated in camp and heard Gerry explain the fears and exhilarations which he had experienced in the jaws of the canyon. And heard, outside, Dettifoss with her eternal roar of defiance.

The Lower Reaches

Now that our planes had proved themselves we could make plans to reach the lower section of the canyon and eventually trace the river to the sea. The microlights would carry some of the gear down river beyond the falls to navigable water, and would then resume their scouting activities. Without this facility the attempt would not have been possible, and it cannot be overstated how important this was to our safety and speed of movement.

Once we had taught ourselves to understand the distortions of scale in rapids and obstructions viewed from the air, which we did initially by comparing the same view by flight and by foot, these aerial reports were to prove of immense value to us time and time again. There were some really huge rapids in the canyon! Some in fact so violent that for security we scouted each section both from the air to get the general picture and then again from the ground to analyse specific hazards.

To put our plans into action required the pruning down of the waterborne expedition and the separating of the other groups. We sent into the current a totally self-supporting unit, consisting of three kayakists, Benoit, Mick and myself. The small raft was deflated and with many of our other stores, stowed in the vehicles which were being driven now by Gudbrandur and Gísli, and which would make their way down the right bank of the river, to rejoin us some days later at the 'exit' of the canyon. The large raft remained, crewed by its skipper, Jeb, the powerful oarsman from Colorado, Bruno and his camera equipment, Jean Jacques with his sound recorders, Robert, that very expert still photographer, Jean-Luc our doctor, dietician and photographer, with all his medical, and photographic gear, and of course the food. We carried sufficient food for five days, which was the expected duration of time before we would liaise with the microlights and vehicles. Gerry and Simon had found a landable area on the left bank and had established a camp site. The microlights however, had not been stacked away, but were kept in readiness for constant surveillance and rescue work, and indeed once again, acted as probes during much of the descent of the river. Stowing the equipment into the raft was a long and careful operation. The value of medical equipment, tents, cooking gear and personal effects was considerable, and the photographic and sound equipment alone was worth some £50,000! The checking of ropes and protective plastic that was made before moving downstream had to be meticulous.

With the kayaks around the raft like a destroyer escort protecting a merchant man during an Atlantic convoy in 1941, she pushed off into the current and into the slacker water by the bank—but only for a moment or two, for she quickly gained the deeper, faster water and within 600 feet (200 m), was amid huge curling waves. These came over the top of the raft and deposited gallons of water into its well. Robert and Jean-Luc put down their cameras in haste and started to bail. The 'destroyers' circled as best they could to be ready to pick up survivors if the 'merchantman' capsized. In this event, survival would have been difficult, for the speed of the water made the possibility of swimming to the bank almost out of the question.

In this water it soon became evident that we were very close to some of the hazards we had seen when we made an initial flight over this section. We had seen a great stopper, across the full width of the river, with a large rock behind it, and then further on, through some wild rapids, we had seen three tremendous waves, which even at our height of 500 feet had called into question the feasibility of running this section. We made the proper decision to pull the raft to the shore. Mick and I stopped close to the bank, stepped out of our kayaks and managed to catch the end of a rope which Jeb had thrown towards us. We hauled the raft into the bank and lifted it onto the rocks.

We made camp. It was an amazing place. The construction of the walls of the canyon resembled a huge pipe organ formed from columnar volcanic rock, and the shape of its curve held the sound of wind and water for a moment until, acoustically enhanced, it echoed across the river and entered our camp. We slept to these sounds and called it the 'Jökulsá Concerto for Organ and Water Music'. We slept well, for the day had been strenuous and had passed very quickly.

The following morning we all set out on foot to scout the canyon immediately below our camp. Two and a half thousand feet (800 m) down the river form changed. The huge waves became flattened, the width between banks reduced and there, almost as a wall across the river, was the great stopper—a dangerous one, to be avoided at all costs.

From the banks we inspected this closer. On the right there was a distinct gap but the violent turbulence there formed dangerous eddies and we would have been foolhardy to attempt to pass. On the left, there was a gap with quieter water which would ordinarily have made passage easier—but directly in our path at the far side of this gap was an immense boulder, almost as big as a house, which we had first seen from the microlight. It would necessitate a swerve to clear it when passing through from the left gap at the stopper. We had another look at the right, but decided that this was the riskier of the two possibilities even for the kayaks. For the raft, there was no question, we would have to go for the left and do the best we could, steerage wise, to avoid the rock beyond. We couldn't risk the raft being caught in the stopper or trapped in the eddy. If they were 'flipped', even if we were lucky enough to rescue all the team, the loss of equipment would have wrecked our expedition.

We scouted further, looking for places where the raft could allow Bruno and Jean-Luc

Overleaf: **The microlight carries two kayaks over the canyon: the barren lava fields either side of the river stretched for miles.**

to disembark for photographic sessions and for movie filming. And then further still for a place where they could be picked up. One pick-up point is not safe enough so it was necessary we thought, to find some more. We found two eventually. We had responsibilities to companies and people who had enabled the expedition to take place. We had promised them a film of the first ever descent of the river and it was essential for our film makers to shoot from the bank as well as from the river. As the canyon snaked its wall along, strange volcanic formations made it seem prehistoric, as indeed it was and it would have been no great surprise for a dinosaur to appear—no wonder our 'pterodactyls' had seemed to belong to the scene.

Snow from previous winters had melted and silky green patches dotted the inner canyon cliff. The fissure opened and closed as we made our way along first wide open gorges and then tight constrictions forming 'S' bends where the walls were almost overhanging, so vertical had they become. Here, on the river, we would find the worst areas, and here, water movements would be unnatural and almost unreadable. We climbed past one such restriction, which was about half a mile in length, and then the canyon widened out again. We were now some 250 feet (80 m) high up, the waves looking immense and absolutely non-stop. And it was from this point that we saw something that would certainly cause problems. The three waves we had originally seen from the air, twice as large as anything else we had seen in the canyon, and completely spanning the river, followed each other through a rapid which looked quite unrunnable even from our high foothold on the wall. They were truly massive, their crests so heavy that they collapsed and fell back down the front surface of the waves. From here, it appeared that any of these waves would have held a kayak in its turbulence and would, without question, turn the raft completely upside down. We scouted two further places for the raft to stop, above this section, for final water level checks. If it really proved impossible we would have to carry the equipment past, along a sandbank at the side of the rapid.

Making our way back towards camp, we again had a look at the fearsome stopper and its long stop, the rock, and we glanced further upstream towards our camp. There was a stretch leading towards the stopper of about 1500 feet (500 m) of very violent rapid—water that we could barely read from its chaotic tumble. We passed alongside this and reached camp, each of us with our thoughts as to how this river was to be navigated. Benoit looked at me and said in his understated French 'Pas mal'. 'Oui' I returned. As we entered camp, Mick asked Jeb about the problems of running the raft through the conditions we described, and in particular against a strong cross wind such as had just arisen within the last hour or so. We decided to wait, and it was not until about 5 o'clock on the evening of 24th August that Benoit, Mick and I squeezed ourselves into our tight cockpits, picked up our paddles and pushed off into the current. The raft was untied, lowered into the river, and with a gentle shove glided into midstream. It appeared easy. Bruno was perched on the back of the raft, Jean-Luc and Robert sat gripping side tubes with one hand, taking photos with the other, and enjoying the ride. From somewhere amidships appeared a periscope but it was a microphone telling us that somewhere in the raft, little Jean Jacques was recording again.

We were approaching the rapids and we knew that we should all be working to the left side of the river to avoid the stopper in the middle and the eddies on the right. Suddenly Jeb screamed 'Bail! Bail! Faster! Faster!' The raft had caught four huge waves and was now full of water and almost uncontrollable. They were well in midstream and if Jeb couldn't manage to pull it over to the left in the next 150 feet (50 m) they would have the choice of the stopper or the virtually unrunnable right aperture—neither of these options being healthy, to say the very least. Jeb was straining on the oars, fighting with every ounce of his tremendous strength, red faced with mixed emotions and effort. Jean-Luc was bailing frantically—for his life, bobbing up and down, throwing water in every direction. Bruno, as ever calm, carried on filming with Jean Jacques recording. Jean-Luc, exhausted, threw· the bucket to Robert who continued to bail with great effort. Closer and closer the raft was being propelled towards the turmoil on the right—it looked as though it would miss the wide stopper and was making direct for the part of the river where we had decided that even the kayaks could not go.

We three kayakists were helpless—we ran the left section backwards, forwards, sideways, any way, to keep the raft in our sight, as she drew inexorably closer to what we were sure was to be a major catastrophe. Mick and I looked at each other—would our months and years of planning end in this place? My mind raced ahead—if they all are thrown into the river, how can we save five men, with three kayaks? What about the gear? I found myself thinking about the film 'Why aren't we filming this?' But, Bruno *was* filming.

Jeb tore at the oars, now so close to the boiling cauldron of the right channel, desperately trying to clear to the left—and then, almost in slow motion it seemed, the raft was sucked sideways into the huge stopper. She submerged, and disappeared. The bow then shot up above the surface and appeared to turn over. My imagination followed it—advanced upon it, and created in my mind an awful capsize, I saw the raft turned over, the men in the river, the equipment lost forever and our hopes and dreams perished in the implacable grip of Jökulsá á Fjöllum. But it was not so! Somehow, and to this day we know not how, somehow, the raft remained right side up and all its occupants were still on board—shaken, wet, exhausted—but on board and very much alive. And of the gear—I dared not imagine—but we had lost only one bailing bucket. I blessed the care with which the raft had been packed—my father would have been proud of our knots!

All this took a second or two which seemed a lifetime, but there was no time to rest, or reflect, for the river took no respite and the raft was scudding downstream, into more danger. Mick, Benoit and I shot down on the left side and overtook the raft, hoping desperately that Jeb would be able to move her over towards the first of the original pull-over points that we had designated for landing Bruno and Jean-Luc. Poised and ready to catch hold of his rope, we watched as our waterlogged inflatable was once again drawn into midstream and to the battle ahead.

We were helpless.

The raft hit a large wave—but, made sluggish by the enormous amount of shipped water, she almost ploughed through it, taking more on board in the process. She reared up, but without her earlier bounce. Slipping and sliding through peaks and troughs, she disappeared from sight only to reappear a little further downstream, completely at the mercy of the water now, with the occupants hanging on for life, and unable to do much more than gasp for breath—and still Bruno filmed! Bruno was incredible!

But we were no longer making a film—this was survival and no-one knew the ending of it. The kayaks were now running this terrible rapid—it was huge and continuous; it was our first ever encounter with such force but we had to stay close to the raft—we

Overleaf:
Left, above: **Benoit, Paul and Mick kayaking in formation between the vertical walls of the canyon. The water looks harmless but the walls create eddies and whirlpools that make it dangerous for swimming.**

Left, below: **Negotiating the first rapid: Mick, Benoit and Paul.**

Right:
'Shifting with precision through the blue cold opposition a one man battalion Aquacade.'
Leon Vander-Molen

Right, top: **Benoit about to put in a turning stroke that will both support and steer him.**

Right, middle: **Mick, using a wooden paddle, kayaking at 45 degrees to the river and looking downriver with an expression of aggression and concentration.**

Right, bottom: **Paul, using a composite paddle, about to come over a wave that is so high he can't see what is the other side. Travelling at about 20 mph he has to be ready either to go into a support stroke or into his next paddle stroke. His eyes are looking downstream although he is at an angle to the river.**

114

would be their only hope if disaster struck. The river got narrower and entered a curve, and the drenched inhabitants of the raft were jolted into action by a shout from Jeb, 'The wall—the wall—we're going into the wall—high side, high side, everyone fend off!' And by a miracle, the raft, pinned to the wall, but undamaged, was *not* tipped sideways and held vertical—the occupants were *not* tipped into the river. Jeb's experience had prevented this and the rapid shift of bodies in the raft had averted a serious accident. A swim in these conditions would have been terminal. And ever present was the thought of those three gigantic waves.

I closed in to the raft—they were OK. I glanced behind me—Benoit had appeared, but there was no sign of Mick. Decision—I would follow the raft and as I returned my gaze, she freed herself from the rocks and looking like a deformed doughnut, she was see-sawing downstream, past the place which ironically enough, we had pin pointed as our second pull-in position. Control was not possible—quite apart from exhaustion, the raft was now barely afloat and completely unresponsive to anything except the wild throws of the river. I waited some minutes, glancing anxiously behind me. There was still no sign of Mick—then Benoit signalled—Mick had been in trouble but was all right and we should stay with the raft. The river here was so fast that in the few moments in which I had waited to find out about Mick, the raft had gone from my view. Two thousand feet (600 m) ahead we caught sight of the doughnut, now deeply dunked and making sluggishly for the next pull-in place. Ten buckets bailed—ten gallons crashed into the raft. All were now bailing with whatever came to hand—and *with* hands as well, but it was a losing battle. For a short while she looked as though she would make the next pull-out place, but once again, the river dragged her into midstream and she became lower in the water.

To our consternation, we were now entering a part of the river which we had only scouted by air. It appeared quite unnavigable. The giant waves were crashing at the entrance to this further reach. Just before we hit the waves, something fell from the raft—in a red sausage-shaped bag it sank below the surface and then floated close enough for me to grab it. I recognised it as sound equipment and vital to our plans—but it was difficult to save it, close as I was to a mad stretch of turbulence, trying with one eye to keep watch on a doughnut while balancing a sausage on my kayak . . . I've had more pleasant meals! I neared the bank and threw the sound sausage to safety. Then I drew level with the raft and saw the occupants bracing themselves for the next attack. Benoit joined me, but still there was no sign of Mick.

We took our breath for a moment, in a slight lessening of the current and looked ahead about 600 feet (200 m) to where the river seemed to disappear over an 'edge'. We knew this wasn't a waterfall from our flights, but it was the sort of formation which marks the commencement of a major rapid. It was the sign telling watermen to stop and look first. The edge underlined the canyon wall which some 2000 feet (600 m) further on turned to the left. Silhouetted on top of this clear sharp edge was our 'expedition' and we watched in horror as it tilted, folded and slithered over and out of sight towards the first of those great waves we knew awaited them.

Benoit and I shot to the bank, sprang out of our boats and rushed up the bank to look at the raft. She was still afloat, more or less and transfixed between the second and third of the giant waves. Assured by the sight of them afloat, we raced back to our kayaks and were there, thankfully, rejoined by Mick. Exhausted, he gasped out that he had had a lot of trouble with his spray deck and had had to empty his canoe. He was very lucky not to have had to swim in these dangerous waters—and he knew it!

Once again, we pushed off, and made for the edge. The raft was out of sight and we knew that what awaited us was untried and untamed—to shoot rapids like these for the first time is a supreme test of skill and experience. To do this in the knowledge that you are the only security for a run-away raft and its crew brings tension to its highest pitch. I could taste the adrenalin as it pumped its message 'Action—now!' We shot over and into chaos—but we couldn't see the raft, and we sped on. The waves were just huge—on my left were dark stoppers. Ahead of me fiercer than a roller coaster, the water threw me high into the air, and as I crashed down hard on to a wave, it twisted me round and up and in and out, and then buried me deep under the brown and green of these sightless rapids. High up, looking down into a vast hollow I was sightless—sightless of the raft which was somewhere in front. Somewhere behind me were Benoit and Mick but in these conditions the sole endeavour is to stay upright and I had no time to seek them out. Somehow I rounded the next bend and could not believe my eyes. Ahead of me was the raft, battered but still unbowed, sitting in an eddy on the left of the river, close to the bank.

The starboard side was submerged in shallow water, but some air remained in the port-side tube. Two oars had been smashed, fortunately without damaging Jeb's hands and arms. There was a great tear about 15 inches (40 cm) long on the edge of the rubber. But most important of all, Jeb, Bruno, Jean-Luc, Jean Jacques and Robert, gasping, drenched and sagging with fatigue were there—and alive. I powered my kayak towards the bank, sprang from it and we hugged each other, as only men who have faced these dangers can. Bruno, intrepid as only he can be, had managed to get a great amount of the dramatic descent of the Jökulsá in his camera, and now, once again, he filmed our joining, and made a picture of the dilapidated raft.

When we checked our stores, we found that we had lost overboard just four cans of beer—Fosters—and so the rapid became known as 'Fosterfoss'. We breathed our gratitude to the spirit of the river which had released us when our chastisement was complete.

The Last Few Miles to the Sea

Camping

We had very mixed feelings. The river had almost broken us and our escape was due not so much to our skill, but to the river's decision to let us go. We were grateful, of course, and glad to be alive. We were relieved that our equipment was, in the main, still in good order and that we would be able to repair the damage and continue. But we were sore about the river—once again one of Iceland's powerful elements had proved just how dangerous it could be. But this time we were determined to have the last word and we talked about our plans for the descent from there to the sea, about 12 miles (20 km) we estimated.

But first, we needed rest—the day had completely drained our reserves of energy. We

Overleaf, main picture:

'Glistening red fish, slithering, challenging, battling
the torrent enemy, triumphantly.'
Leon Vander-Molen

The raft begins to get into trouble and the kayaks move in.

Overleaf, left, top: **Paul's kayak disappears in the turbulent water.**

Overleaf, left, middle: **Now the 18-foot raft is completely hidden by waves. Note both kayaks keeping close to it and both kayakists showing the same stroke.**

Overleaf, left, middle: **The raft begins to take in water.**

Overleaf, left, bottom: **Robert looking exhausted has photographed the entire incident; the deflated raft sags in the water.**

were wet, cold and tired. And very, very hungry. Where we had found the washed up raft was in fact an ideal place for us to set up camp. Some twenty feet above the rocky riverside was a broad flat area, just ideal for putting up our tents. This camping ground was in the shelter of a higher part of the canyon wall, which when we climbed it led not only to a little dirt track which then led eventually to the only access road on the left of the canyon, but also offered us a fine flat area on which our microlight could land. There was an additional bonus—not far away was a lonely ranger's hut.

We decided then, at about 5 o'clock, that we would put up our tents in the lee of the canyon wall and get ourselves sorted out. Our tents, having being damaged by the blizzards on Vatnajökull, had been carefully repaired by Mick and Jeb, who had made them water and wind proof by a combination of stitching and bonding, using canoe tape inside and out. These tents came from a company called Ultimate and had the name Phazer Dome. They consisted of six panels, joined at the centre, which, when laid down, opened out rather like the petals of a flower. At the outside perimeter of each panel is a flap which is large enough to load with earth, rocks or snow to hold the tent down and in addition, somewhat to the centre of each panel is an attachment for a guy line and peg. Three fibreglass batons have to be slipped into sheaths in certain panels and this has the effect of pulling the tent into a dome shape, which with some juggling at the ends of the batons, becomes very stable. There is an inner tent and a ground sheet all in one. Entrance is through a zipped opening in a panel and then through the inner door and a mosquito net. They were excellent for their purpose and would have been perfect had it not been for the quite extraordinary weather on the glacier. Each would accommodate two or three men, and our expedition seemed to pair off naturally—Jeb and Mick sharing one, Gerry and I in another, Bruno and Jean Jacques together and so on.

We had dragged the poor old raft on to the rocks and we now squeezed all the water from its drowned tube and left it to dry. While Benoit and Jean Jacques went on a mission of rescue along the canyon walls to retrieve the 'sound sausage' which I had cast ashore during the mêlée in the rapids, we got ourselves organised into a respectable camp, and like boy scouts, got a camp fire going. This may not seem much in itself, but in Iceland there are very few trees and thus very little wood. A camp fire was a rare luxury. Ours blazed away merrily, courtesy of our broken oars and some rotten palings we discovered lying near the hut. Definitely a bonus.

Our comfort was complete when, by the light of the fire, we downed tinned hot dogs, meat balls, eggs, spaghetti and sundry other goodies. Mick had brought with him a cooking utensil, a Chinese wok, and I incurred his wrath the following morning when having made a marvellous job of cleaning this dish with wire wool and soap, I proudly presented it to him: 'Here you are,' I said expectantly, 'It hasn't looked as clean as that for years!'

'Oh, thanks Paul—it's taken you two minutes to completely destroy the surface which I have been building up for over two years—thanks a lot!' was Mick's tart rejoinder, followed by a severe lecture on the theory of 'wokking'. Apparently, they are not to be washed or scraped, but must be nurtured into a mature patina. Privately, I thought he might have been more grateful—after all it had been in an awful mess the night before, and now you could have shaved in it—such is life!

Our wanderers had returned with the 'Sound Sausage' in good order and joined us for food, and then, to our delight, Gerry and Simon flew in, having spotted our camp on one of their routine surveys of the river. The warden of the hut, a superb Icelandic girl, radioed Grímstadir and this eventually led to contact with the vehicles which later joined us at our site. The hut, with its attractions (!) tempted some to make for it—others camped! We were now all together again, and glad to have the chance to recoup our strength.

The following morning was Robert's birthday and I cooked him a special breakfast to mark the occasion. The day dawned sunny and we began to luxuriate in the rare leisure. The raft which had dried out, had now to be completely deflated, which took the efforts of most of us sitting and lying on it. We made a note to use suction from a vehicle, generator or even a microlight engine next time. When suitably flattened, our raft was rolled into a snake and taken to a nearby village, some 30 miles (50 km) away, by road, where there was a man, we had been told, who had a boat and oars. Jeb had reckoned that repairs would take us about two days and as it happened, he was not far out. Having sorted out some gear in the village, they then returned to camp to complete the mending of the raft, which was done finally with a mixture of stitching, bonding and re-inforcing with flaps. And the time wore on for those engaged thus. Others took the beautiful weather as the opportunity to film the scenery, to scout the rapids ahead on foot and in the air, and to take the microlights further along the river, almost to its mouth. And some of us just rested and reflected.

That night, some of us were in tents—and there was still that attractive hut! We awoke from our second night much refreshed and full of our plans to complete the river descent down to a bridge which officially, was the end of Jökulsá á Fjöllum. From here it splits into two smaller streams which then join the Arctic Ocean. The raft was dry, solid and (we hoped) water worthy. We inflated her, took her to the rocks and with care, lowered her into the water, testing carefully for leaks. She was good, and appeared none the worse for her ordeal, much to the credit of her designers and to our repair team—notably Jeb. She would await us in this quiet piece of water, for we had scores to settle with the river . . .

Backtrack

We had decided to retrace our journey 2500 feet (800 m) back up above our camp site and to re-run part of the rapid that had given us such a hard time two days ago. Then the river had been in control—now maybe we could take charge. Mick, Benoit and I set off on foot up the canyon. The microlights went aloft and circled around, eventually making towards the sea, while the trucks, with the heaviest of our gear, started off to the bridge. Camp was closed down. Some of the others followed we three kayakists to take films and photographs and perhaps, just to watch. The weather remained perfect. It was towards the latter part of the morning when we finally arrived at our destination, which was just below the part of the river where we had encountered those three giant waves, nearly three long days ago. We had climbed up and down the walls, carrying our kayaks and now we had to lower them by ropes to the water's edge. We intended to go through the two major rapids which were now ahead of us, rejoin the raft and continue as a flotilla towards the sea and journey's end.

But today the river had changed. Where days ago there had been quieter stretches, we

Overleaf:
Left, top: **A better day—the loaded raft and its 'ghost driver' negotiating new rapids with ease.**

Left, bottom: **Paul, Benoit and Mick negotiating rough waters; Paul rolling to get himself out of difficulty.**

Right, top: **Camping on the river bend after the raft accident.**

Right, below: **The red of the microlight is echoed in the lava rock behind as it flies in to take a closer look at the 'Man and Woman' rock.**

now saw deadly stoppers. And in some places where there *had* been stoppers, we now found manageable waves. The water, generally was lower—as we had expected from our flow charts, for we were now very late in August and the ice melt had reduced considerably. Having agreed a security plan, we set off.

Benoit, first to lead, kayaked along the agreed route and pulled over to the bank some 600 feet (250 m) downstream. He signalled with his paddle and indicated whether the next canoe should go left or right. Mick followed this signal, while Benoit remained in wait, ready to effect a rescue if Mick got into difficulties, and then on a signal from Mick, I followed on. We continued this leapfrog assault on the rapids for some time, until we rounded a left bend in the river. Here the river had speeded up and there were dangerous eddies on the right. It was close to here that the raft had been pinned against the canyon wall and had then scraped along, narrowly avoiding disaster. We avoided disaster in our kayaks giving the wall a very wide berth. Mick yelled and pointed at it as we approached, 'No swimming there—not a chance in that!' We nodded agreement and sped on. Soon we came to another bend, to the right and this time with some sand banks.

Swimming

I was now in the lead and after a further 1200 feet (400 m) in white water, I pulled in to the right, just above a very major rapid, where I could see huge curling waves and savage stoppers. It looked a hard run indeed. I watched for sight of Benoit behind me and could just see his head bobbing up and down in waves, and it made me realise the sheer size of the water I had just gone through—and the next section looked worse! Eventually Benoit closed in on me and when we had reached the comparative safety of our holding place, we signalled to Mick, who had been waiting on the left bank. He set off and quickly entered the central stream of the rapid. I saw from the corner of my eye that the others on the bank were filming the scene and thought to myself, this should really make an exciting sequence. Little did I know what was to follow!

Mick disappeared—I assumed he had been caught by one of those large stopper waves. Long seconds passed and then I saw his head bobbing up and down in the water. I saw no danger—moments before, this is just how Benoit had appeared in the water as he sped to join me. And then suddenly I saw Robert on the bank cross his arms and wave frantically, it was our agreed danger signal—something must be wrong! I looked back towards the river and saw Mick's paddle seem to leap from the water. I watched holding my breath, and then Mick appeared again, half out of his canoe, the spray deck ripped off and water filling the aperture. He was fighting for breath and being sucked under by each wave and any moment he would be dragged from the canoe completely. As the torrent swept him down even closer and closer to the next wild rapid, we could see him weakening—but as long as we had sight of him, there was a chance of rescue—we had to get to him *now*. As we watched, waiting our chance, the canoe was torn from his grasp and as man and boat separated, we lost all sight of him.

Using what slack water we could find, close to the bank, Benoit and I made our way upstream at the fastest speed we could muster. We searched the water with our eyes, willing Mick to appear, almost despairing when there was no sight of him and then, to our everlasting relief, we saw him, struggling, trying to swim towards the right bank. But he was exhausted—his strokes were slower and slower and we saw him fighting for his life. Benoit, with superb mastery of the water, chose his moment and darted into the fierce waves, just close enough for Mick to grab the V-rope at his stern. Using every ounce of his strength, Benoit literally dragged Mick into shallow water, where there was a boulder garden of rocks at the start of the next rapid. Mick, regaining his feet, gave us a wry grin—his resilience was remarkable, and when in a few moments we judged it safe for us to leave him, Benoit and I went off in search of the lost kayak and paddle.

They were now way ahead of us, in the stretch of rapid that we had intended to navigate in company with the raft in the afternoon. It was water we had scouted but not run. But now we had no choice—we had to have that canoe. We saw it, being tossed about, thrown up and sucked down, but when we closed on it, it seemed to attack us, almost like a wild fish, maddened by the river, snapping at its would-be captors. Approaching it with some caution, and then losing it, and then gaining on it, we pursued our quarry for 1200 feet (400 m) magically contriving to stay upright in the crashing turmoil of water. Then quite suddenly it was drawn into an eddy almost opposite the place where our raft had been thrown out of the river, and our camp site of the previous nights.

This eddy was dangerous. We approached it as close as we could and were turned and had to roll and were thrown back and then drawn in. It was tricky work, but I managed to grab the paddle which had partnered its kayak into the eddy, just as the canoe moved downstream again. I made a javelin of the paddle and reached the left bank with my first throw. We were now 600 feet (200 m) past our camp site and deep into the new rapid. From the low seat of my kayak I saw waves 8 – 10 feet high. I caught glimpses of the leaping fish ahead and judging it to be safe, darted in to grab its rope. It fought me with all the strength of a bucking bronco but I held on to its bridle and bit by bit I drew it upside down on to the deck of my own canoe, realising as I did so, that I was now going down the rapid backwards. Benoit stayed close to guide me. Hauling hard, I fought it to a standstill and using the bows of my boat as a fulcrum, pivoted Mick's drowning canoe to empty it of water. This is the technique known as 'X' rescue in kayaking. I rolled it upright and alongside, and then, holding on to it tightly, struggled as best I could towards the right bank. Thankfully I reached a quieter eddy and, joined by Benoit, we shunted the canoe onto some gravel, and breathed hard. We both needed a rest.

And with the resumption of normal breathing came the resumption of normal thinking. First the chilling thought that we had nearly lost Mick. And then, the realisation that we now had Mick on the right of the river. But we, with his canoe (and upstream, his paddle), were all on the left. When we had got our strength back, we carried his kayak back up the bank just opposite our camp site and while I ferried it across the river, Benoit went off to retrieve the paddle. Mick, meanwhile, had been clambering along on foot and arrived as we landed. The others of the team, who had been filming and agonising at the dramatic events of the morning, slowly arrived at our meeting place and we restored our spirits with some lunch and river talk.

Finals

Jökulsá á Fjöllum is an enigma—its moods and changes are frequent and extravagant

Overleaf: **The Icelandic Life Saving Association's hut makes a bold splash of colour against the ridged mountains in the background.**

and during our journey on its broad back it had fought with us in unabated fury. Now we were afloat once more and about to make the final descent to the sea. Ahead of us was a great rapid, which earlier that day had brought us to a high pitch of activity and called into play all our skills as kayakists. Would Jökulsá challenge us yet again? Or would it permit us to go forward to our journey's ending?

These were some of my thoughts when, in the afternoon, suitably refreshed and rested, we set off on our final leg. We anticipated that the wild rapid into which we had penetrated earlier to retrieve Mick's canoe, would severely tax our flotilla and that the raft with Jeb, Jean Jacques and Robert on board would have great difficulty in passing through. Whether we had learned sufficient of this rapid in our morning 'trial' to be able to find the best routes, or whether in the few hours that had elapsed some subtle change came upon the river, I cannot tell. I can only say that we navigated this very difficult stretch of water with confidence and success. There were no incidents of danger and we were able to enjoy the bright, though cold, weather and to admire the beauty of the last few miles of the canyon, while Bruno and Jean-Luc took films from the canyon walls.

We set off well, skirting a small eddy that was on the left, just outside our camp and from then on it was almost plain sailing, as though we were on a different rapid. In a way we were, because we had better choices of routes than we had had in the morning chase. The rapid extended for some few miles and then we glided upon calmer waters. And it is here that some reflection might be given to the men in the raft, and in particular Robert Grégoire, our still photographer. To sit perched upon the edge of the raft taking shots from all angles does not seem impressive in calm water, but to continue this operation in rapids of the most violent turbulence, with little heed for danger and while maintaining a steady camera hand, called for professionalism of the highest order. Many absolutely beautiful pictures were taken in this way and there is no doubt that the results of the expedition from a photographic point of view were greatly enhanced by his expertise and courage. Aged now 42 since his birthday in camp, Robert, a tall spare person, with a quiet voice and reserves of hidden power, which the observer could detect occasionally, was precise and ordered in manner. He attempted to achieve order and serenity in all that he did, even when we confronted him with chaotic conditions, and very often, amazingly, he succeeded. His photographic stance was influenced by his experience in producing advertising photographs and the high standard of his art in this sphere was attested to by the wonderful shots he was able to provide for our sponsors, both as scenic offerings and pure shots of dramatic action. With Jean-Luc, who has a natural all round talent for picture taking, we were well served by our photographic team. The English was somewhat basic in Robert's case but minor frustrations were assuaged by his mature temperament. We got on well and he participated fully, though, as might have been expected from one so much older than the rest of us, he needed from time to time to be convinced that were we making the right decisions.

Jeb, in the raft, we have spoken about at length—he was a power house and reliable in danger—a large extrovert Colorado man. The third member of the raft was Jean Jacques. He never appeared without his recording microphone and it was almost as if this was an extra arm—he never lost his nerve and he never lost his good humour, this tough little man from Morocco.

The river carried us along on her ample bosom—we were approaching the end of the canyon and could see the widening of the stream, and the change of ground to the sandy plain. There was more plant life—the volcanic lava scape seemed to change to a softer, more rolling outline, and the river took its cue from the land, and rolled, though still flowing fast. But not quite so fast. We paddled on, but it was a time for reflection. Where had we been? What had we done? Had we achieved all we had set out to do? It was a time to recall with gratitude the escapes we had had from disaster . . . so near and yet, thankfully, so far. We all thought of what we had put into these full days and wondered what we had got out of them.

For each of us it must have been something different—and it is hard for me to say what would be in the minds of my brothers on this river. For me, there was the realisation of a dream—we had proved my microlight theory. For Bruno, and the other men of pictures there would have been the satisfaction of knowing that a superb film was in the can and that we had an enormous number of photographs and recordings. For Mick and Benoit, the joy of their river expertise and of the Ice Caves, which would live in their memories for a long time. For Jeb, the exhilaration of his days aboard the raft, the companionship and communion of the river. For our fliers, the realisation of new techniques and the opening up of new boundaries . . . and for our Icelandic friends, the thrill of participating in the assault upon their mighty glaciers and rivers.

Soon, immersed in our thoughts, we saw the bridge approaching, where we met with the vehicles and the microlights. We rested for a while and talked of our exploits. We had been travelling for 45 days, it was now September 2nd and we had left London on 18th July. We had sailed some 500 miles (800 km) and driven, walked, flown, skied, kayaked and rafted between 2000 and 3000 miles (3–5000 km). In this travel we had received upwards of 17 punctures, we had ruined 5 propellers, repaired 4 exhausts, lost 4 oars and lacerated our float. We had 10 hours of film and over 11,000 photos. The Ever Ready van had provided us with 300 batteries at Newcastle. We had used over 500 in all! We had almost lost 4 tents in the blizzard, we had squashed a generator, wrecked a skiddoo and done some damage to the suspension of an Olís truck. We had consumed about half a tonne of foodstuffs. We had used very little soap—and we had used about 120 rolls of toilet paper. But most of all, we had been permitted the use of beautiful Iceland and had exercised to the full, the generous assistance and goodwill of our many friends in Iceland whom we remember with affection and gratitude.

For the last one or two miles to the sea, we kayaked silently, but with exhilaration. While we still reflected on our adventure, we saw the low evening sun, reflected in the quiet surf of the ocean, and as we reached journey's end and jubilantly paddled into the sea, we discovered that the water at the mouth of Jökulsá á Fjöllum, and for a distance of several hundred feet out, was clean river water amid the salt of the ocean—Jökulsá's last gesture of invincibility. Yet, we had made it—we had broken through the barriers—it was Iceland Breakthrough!

Epilogue

The Presidential Reception

On 3rd September, 1983 we arrived in Reykjavík and took the opportunity to meet friends and thank sponsors and to tie up loose ends. And to get our breath back.

One or two of the team had commitments and went home, but most of us stayed on in Iceland for a few days—we were due to catch the ferry *Edda* on the 7th or the 9th, so we were at leisure. A famous Icelandic gentleman, Omar Ragnarsson, had been very helpful to us in setting up the expedition. He is celebrated in Iceland as a T.V. personality, rally driver, pilot, comedian, cameraman and more. We of the team wished in some way to express our thanks to the Icelandic people and we thought that it would be wonderful if we could have the opportunity of speaking to the President of Iceland. Getting to see the President of any country is not easy and so we spoke to Omar Ragnarsson, who had always seemed to be able to get things done. When we asked his advice, he pursed his lips and shook his head but within a very short space of time, he contacted us again and we were told to our delight that the President had agreed to see us in two days' time. Thrilled and delighted we decided that we should make her a presentation to mark the occasion.

We had the propeller of the first microlight to fly over Dettifoss and on the hub of this we had attached an engraved plaque of silver. Kári's friend, the pilot Ivar, who was professionally an engraver, produced a beautiful design very quickly and when finished, it had the engraved signatures of each team member superimposed above an outline map of Iceland showing our route and with a message of thanks from the Iceland Breakthrough Team to the People of Iceland.

We retrieved our two original vehicles from the customs shed, where we had deposited them on arrival and found that the number plates had been removed for security reasons. We then had to go to another office to get them, where we encountered some bureaucratic delay and in fact did not get them until the day of the Presidential audience. We were all dressed up in Alafoss sweaters, combed and shining and of course very excited. There was no time to fix the number plate on the car, so we bundled it into the back window, and set off for the President's home. We had not gone far when we were flagged down by two police cars. Forced to stop, we saw a lady officer get out of one car and a man from the other. In forceful language they demanded to know what we thought we were doing driving a car without number plates—we were not to proceed. We were now short of time to get to the President. We tried to explain that we had an important meeting to go to but they were not inclined to take much notice of this, until we said 'Look—we must go, we've got an audience with the President,' and to prove our words unwrapped the propeller and showed them the inscription. Their incredulity was a sight to behold but as it dawned on them that we were telling the truth, they signalled for us to start up and then acted as our escort all the way to the President's home. Our cavalcade arrived in time and entered a long drive towards an elegant house. We had

Left: 'The Icelanders are above all a race of poets, inspired perhaps by the nature of the country ...'

sufficient time to make sure we were all spruced up. We wore expedition ties and rather felt, as we inspected each other, that we looked 'posh'. That is except for Jeb's footwear! In the bustle of getting to the audience, Jeb had forgotten about his shoes and was wearing a succession of holes surrounded by the remnants of what must have been at some time past, a pair of trainer plimsolls—they were quite disreputable and definitely not Presidential wear.

'Don't worry too much' said Mick, 'I've heard that the Lady President is a very friendly person.'

Jeb's response to this was 'Does that mean she'll let us check the fridge for beer?'

Feeling rather nervous, we walked to the door and were let in by a young lady. We entered a beautiful hall in this very impressive house where there was an abundance of oak and a sweeping staircase and we were asked to sign the visitors' book. We were shown into a reception area, where we saw President Vigdís Finnbogadóttir waiting to receive us. This beautiful lady with fair hair and piercing blue eyes greeted each of us with a handshake and spoke to us in fluent English and French. We were offered sherry and some biscuits and during the next hour she asked us questions and we told her of our expedition. She said that she had followed the story and she called us 'Adventurers of the Highlands.'

I produced the propeller and read to her the inscription. She thanked us for it and said it was the most original gift she had ever received. It led her to tell us that she was very interested in flying and there followed some discussion of microlighting. We had been informed that there was to be no photography but Robert, resourceful as ever, had brought a camera and asked her permission in French. She graciously gave her assent and we were able to make a record of these proud moments. The President was very informal and put us all at our ease, but Jeb was rather self-conscious about his shoes and when she turned to us and said 'May I ask you a personal question?' he was in considerable discomfort and looked down at his feet with embarrassment. I must admit, we all wondered what she was going to ask and were much relieved when we heard 'How much did the whole expedition cost you?'

Eventually the audience was at an end and we thanked her for her courtesy and through her, the people of Iceland for their friendship, and left the President of Iceland deciding on the most appropriate place to display the propeller.

The Lessons Learned

There were lessons to be learned from Iceland Breakthrough. It was, in terms of the use made of some of the equipment, two or three years ahead of its time, and rather in the nature of an experiment. In particular, it pointed towards future developments of the microlight and techniques evolved to expand its use as a perfect exploration work horse. But before talking of the future, let me bring out some points in relation to the expedition itself. Right at the outset it had been my intention to try to make the best expedition film, and I had certain ideas about avoiding what I thought were inherent mistakes made in other films of this genre by including in the plan:

● A team prepared to make an expedition and film at the same time, with no 'purists'.
● An integral camera crew, thus obviating the conflict of direction.

● Greater 'audience participation' to be introduced by means of 'point of view' camera work using specialised techniques to bring the viewer actually to feel that he is part of the scene.

● The use of live, direct sound for atmosphere.

● The intermingling of a variety of disciplines—kayaking, microlighting, climbing, rafting and so on, to keep interest at a high pitch.

● The study of colour for the best imagery.

● The careful use of continuity linkage a) through personalities b) through equipment, i.e. same clothes throughout scenes, and same kayaks always around.

● Sufficient time for filming within the scale of the expedition.

● The use of the microlight as a vehicle for filming, with its excellent all round vision.

● Adequate 'back-up' services for the camera crew requirements.

● The longer term consideration of post production features, such as a) maps, b) commentary, c) music.

All of these facets were involved in the planning, and the success or otherwise of the venture will indicate the degree to which we learned how to adapt and use these principles amid the excursions and alarms of the journey.

Results have prompted some work to be initiated in microlights. For instance, the trike system can now be obtained with 'in wheel' brakes, and a better shock absorption system is in design. The wing has been reshaped and should now offer a steeper rate of climb and descent for use in contained areas. Work is being done on the drive system, engines, and exhausts and there is a possibility of using a four-stroke engine for more reliability. The floats have been redesigned—they can now be produced with compartments, each acting as a watertight bulkhead and each with its own inspection panel so that the pilot can check the water content before taking off. The rudders have been redesigned and a better linkage arrangement put together. Thanks to an initial idea from Gerry, it is now possible to obtain a float which will fix on to the undercarriage without first having to remove the wheels, thus saving a considerable amount of spanner work.

Other plans in the pipeline are an extended fuel system allowing longer flights, and, with a view to the aeronautical/nautical concept, the wing will be able to fold centrally thus reducing the 'stack-away' space to half its original length. On a personal note, I would like to see some promotion of the following ideas:

● A versatile power unit which could act as the engine of the microlight, or be removed and converted for use with a water screw as a sort of outboard motor for the raft. Or could, locked into a suitable stand, operate as a generator for lighting and for power tools, or as a pump/extractor for the air in rafts, and maybe for heating also. Thus an expedition could carry two of these machines and be very, very self sufficient.

● On the score of the undercarriage of microlights, I would like to see a scheme in which a system of wheels could alternate with floats by means of a lever in control of the pilot, or similarly, an adaption for converting skis to wheels and back again, by pilot control.

● And then, in the field of kayak design, I feel that it might be possible to arrange an accessory for use on the bottom of a kayak which would convert it into a float. If this could be so, then one step in the above arrangements could be cut out, thus making the whole idea even more streamlined.

● In the photographic field, we were able to perform *point of view* filming by use of small 16 mm minicameras enclosed in a waterproof container of fibreglass. There might well be other types of camera more suited to thus purpose, where one idea is to fit the camera to a kayak or microlight so that the viewer is actually in the air, or down in the water when he sees the film. One such use, with the minicam fixed by a bracket on to the helmet of a kayakist, gave the viewer the actual sensation of canoeing down a rapid. With its battery placed for counterbalance, this weighed about 3 lb (1 kg) and we were concerned about the safety in eskimo rolls and during enforced swims. Actually it caused little or no problem and it was a very cheap adaption. Perhaps some such arrangement could be made as a production model at some time. New ways of obtaining views in filming are being sought constantly, as in the method of fixing a camera to the front of a kayak and having a remote control system to rotate it upon its axis for all-round filming. This can be very costly, and we overcame this on our expedition by tying two canoes together, bows to bows, using the V ropes and toggles which we had there for safety purposes, for one canoeist to paddle while a cameraman sat in the other one with complete freedom of view. There is an illusion of filming from within the cockpit itself and this once again, 'brings the viewpoint of the expedition'. This novel method of solving the problem might give rise to further work on methods of camera control.

Quo Vadis?

And so to the question *Quo Vadis?* Whither do we go? Members of Iceland Breakthrough Team feel that new techniques of exploration and film making have had their tentative beginnings in our adventure, and we feel privileged to have initiated such ideas.

* * *

Footnote by Jack Vander-Molen
As I wrote this book in close collaboration with my son Paul, I followed faithfully the ethics and ideas he expounded while he told me the story of the expedition. Sadly he has gone from us, but those who knew him and loved him will take his lead and try to continue his work.

Paul Vander-Molen, the third child of four, was born in north-west London on 23 December 1956. He was educated at Hendon High School up to A levels and then proceeded to obtain an Honours Degree in Mechanical Engineering and Design at the Middlesex Polytechnic.

Early on in his life it became apparent that Paul had exceptional qualities of resourcefulness and self reliance; that he was an innovator and that he enjoyed competitive success and foreign travel. At just 12 years of age he entered an Adventure Challenge Competition at an International Scouts Camp and won first prize over some 2000 other entrants—the prize—a two-week trip to Helsinki!

This first success was repeated many times when he participated (often at competition level) in pole vaulting, wind surfing, surf boarding, dinghy sailing, water skiing, sub-aqua diving, skiing, hang-gliding, microlighting and kayaking. Kayaking, however, was his main sport (in 1978 he reached Division One in the canoeing union) and was to be the prime motivation for his later expeditions. His activities took him to Austria, Germany, America, Italy, Spain, France, Finland, Alaska and Iceland.

The first major expedition Paul organised was in 1981 when he led a team of kayakists and rafters down the river Alsek in Alaska. Under the title 'Valley of Ice' this expedition was extensively reported by Thames TV in England and Antenne II in France. Paul had always taken a great interest in helping disabled people, encouraged no doubt by the work of his father, a well known professional Orthotist, and he put into practice his ideas of helping them when he took a team of variously disabled people and helpers to France, where they kayaked down the Dordogne and Ariège rivers. This expedition prompted Paul to design a one-armed paddle, which has proved very useful.

His skills as an innovator showed themselves also at college and work where he designed and made a prototype model of a satellite stabilising system which was shown on the 'Tomorrow's World' television programme, gained a European Patent for the invention of a special type of centrifugal clutch and obtained a World Patent for his invention of a headlamp adjusting system.

A Fellow of the Royal Geographic Society, Paul received the Ness Award for 'Expedition Leadership and Introduction of Microlight Aircraft as an Expedition Tool'. This followed shortly after his return from his last expedition, Iceland Breakthrough, which with its book and the film which will eventually be shown all over the world, was undoubtedly Paul's most ambitious and successful project.

Paul became ill with leukemia shortly after completing this expedition, but with treatment was restored to health and was able to see the film through to completion and to celebrate its being awarded 2 gold medals at the 1985 French Film Festival and its purchase by British, French and American television.

Sadly, Paul contracted the disease again in January 1985, within days of finding a publisher for this book. But with the energy, optimism and dynamism that was so typical of his approach to life, he organised the writing of this book and working closely with his father, from his hospital bed, gained great pleasure and satisfaction from reading the final manuscript.

A kind and caring man, Engineer, Inventor, Explorer, Athlete, Film Director, Author and Poet, who lived life to the full, who treasured friendships and loved laughter, he would wish the final words to be

'Better by far you should forget and smile
Than you should remember and be sad.'

Paul Nicholas Vander-Molen died, aged 28, on 15 May 1985.

Appendix

Equipment Taken

1. Kayaks

6 kayaks
10 paddles
6 spray decks
5 crash hats
12 paddle jackets
Expanded polystyrene blocks
Buoyancy bags (4 per boat)
Deck lines, toggles
Waterproof bags for storage
Back straps
3 buoyancy aids
3 compressed air life jackets
Throw bags x 4

Repair Kit (specifically Kayak)
Fibreglass matting
1 gallon resin
Catalyst
Mixing cups
Sand paper
Scissors
Files (round and flat)
Spare cord
Canoe tape
Spare end toggles
Aluminium plate
Spare foot rests
Nuts and bolts
Hacksaw blades
Gaz burner
Neoprene sections (and glue/solvent)
Spare expanded polystyrene
Hand drill and drill bits
Pop rivets and gun

2. Rafts

1 Avon Professional inflatable raft 16 ft
1 aluminium paddle frame

Set fixing straps
2 oars (10 ft), (+ 2 spare)
Aluminium waterproof cases (ammunition
   boxes)
Waterproof bags
Ropes
Bailing buckets
Two large hanging nets for equipment
Straps for packing raft into motorised
   hang-glider
5 compressed-air life jackets
6 crash hats
6 buoyancy aids

Repair Kit and Spares
Sand paper, various grades
Solvent to prepare surface
Needle and cotton (special)
Repair patches
Spare 'D' loops
Bonding liquid (neoprene glue)
Chalk
Spare valves
Spare cord
2 spare oars

3. Skiing

8 pairs skis
6 pairs seal skins
12 pairs snow goggles
6 pairs ski goggles
8 pairs ski poles
8 pairs ski boots

4. Climbing

1 90-m rope (9 mm)
3 45-m ropes (11 mm)

8 harnesses
Ice axes and hammers
Assorted nuts/chocks
1 pair Jumars
1 pair Etriers
20 ice screws
Pitons
12 slings
20 carabiners
8 Rucksacks
1 45-m rope (5 mm)

5. Caving Equipment

Waterproof bags (use raft and canoe bags)
8 crash hats (use kayak crash hats)
Ropes (use climbing ropes)
Ice screws (as climbing)
Special head lighting apparatus with
    batteries
Oxygen masks with oxygen supply
Ice axes (as climbing)
Waterproof outers (wet suits or sail boat
    outers)
Life jackets (as rafting equipment)
Torches, waterproof
Flares
Special lighting (Gaz lantern)

6. Specialised Clothing

8 wetsuits (long-john type)
8 wetsuits (jacket type)
10 pairs wet suit boots
19 pairs Helly Hansen type inner sock
15 pairs of Damart underclothes
12 Ozee jackets for glacier
12 special SP27 jackets
12 pairs Helly Hansen-type gloves
Woollen hats for glacier
12 warm Icelandic sweaters
20 special expedition 'T' shirts
Waterproof outclothes for caving and sail
    boat

7. Microlights

(All equipment is for each microlight)

2 fully equipped microlights (Sprint wing,
    motor, Trike)
1 protective bag for wing and machine
1 fuel tank (+ one spare)
2 spare taped propellers
2 helmets (see kayak equipment)
1 compass
1 altimeter
1 r.p.m. gauge
1 paddle (split paddle from kayak)
2 goplane floats
2 manually inflating life jackets (see rafting
    equipment)
2 smoke flares
2 balaclavas (personal fit)
2 radios and recharging kits, emergency
    transmitter, sonic intercom
Spares: spark plugs, prop tape nuts bolts
    aluminium tube, carburettor wing latts,
    piston, rings, cables, engine
Quantity of sponge rubber
Rope
1 box filtrate oil
4 carabiners
Strobe Ident. (emergency transmitter)
First aid kit (small portable)
1 splash guard

8. Land vehicles

1 Datsun pick-up truck
1 Ford Econoline
1 small trailer with adaptable frame
1 large trailer with adaptable frame
Two V.H.F. sets set to expedition frequency
Two sets of snow chains
1 large hand-type vertical jack
De-icer and scraper
Spare fuel tank
Fire extinguisher (one per vehicle)
Portable windscreen
Lengths of rope

Spares
Spare types
Spark plugs (heater if Diesel)
Half shafts
Starter motor
Fuses
Carburettor (injectors if Diesel)
Fan belts
Nuts and bolts
Spare coil

Fuel pump
Set of points
Accelerator cable
Brake fluid
Wires (high and low tension)
Oil and containers (engine and gear box)
Spare keys
Foot pump
Funnel and filter
Tow rope
2 tyre levers
10 spare inner tubes

9. Cooking (Assuming 12 people throughout project)

Two phases a) on the glacier, b) off the
   glacier
2 large pressure cookers
2 large frying pans
2 heating stoves (2 burners each)
Set of billies
12 sets of cutlery (knives, forks, spoons)
12 bowls
12 mugs
12 plates
Set sharp knives
Large spoons
3 tin openers
Matches (or lighters)
Table for eating/cooking etc
Eating tent
Water containers
Purification tablets
Washing-up bowl
Sponges and drying up towels
Brillo pads and Fairy Liquid
Bottle opener
Plastic containers for opened food
Silver (aluminium) foil
Spade
Toilet facilities
1 Chinese wok plus accessories

10. Camping (based on team of 12)

5 dome tents, 3 places each
3 smaller two-man tents (2 Phoenix, 1
   Jean-Luc)
12 close cell foam mats

12 sleeping bags (synthetic)
3 down-type sleeping bags
Lengths of rope for drying clothes
Rubber mallet
Fold-up spade

Spares and Repairs
24 lightweight pegs
Tent repair kit: sewing equipment (see raft),
   patches, tape, guys
Spare tent poles

11. Photographic Equipment (Film not included)

Nikon FE
Nikon F2
Nikon FM
Motors
Canon F1
Canon NF1
Canon FTD
Canon AE1
Motors
250 photo special back. (one for Canon
and one for Nikon)
2 flash
2 x 24 mm
17 mm
2 x 35 mm
2 x 50 mm
135 mm
100 mm
500 mm
2 x 300 mm
Tripod
Doubler
Noctinikkor 58 mm (1,2)
Nikon 15 mm (or 16 mm super wide angle)
Teleobjectif 600 mm (Nikon)
Radio system for pressing button
3 waterproof cameras (24 x 36 format) type
Fuji Baroudeur, with lens.
Underwater flash Sunpak
2 waterproof bags with lens glass for Nikon
2 waterproof containers for equipment
2 carrying bags special protection and heat
   conservation
Batteries for: cameras, motors, portable
   flash, underwater flash light meters
Light meter for underwater use
Umbrella

12. Cinema

Film
Arriflex SR1 High Speed, 10:100 Zeiss
Arriflex SR1
Waterproof casing for Arriflex
9.5 mm lens
300 mm lens with doubler (600 m)
Two tripods, light with fluid heads
Bell and Howell clockwork
Bolex Clockwork
1 mini cam in water-tight case charger and
    spare battery
Light system
Lithium batteries
Filters
Spare cartridges for cameras
Light cell
Spare clockwork mini cam
Fittings for kayak
Fittings for helmet
Waterproof cases for all carrying cases

Sound
Nagra 4
Nagra SN

13. Tool Kit

1 set ring spanners
1 set open-ended spanners
1 set of pipe spanners
Complete socket set (metric, UNC,
    Whitworth)
1 set flat screw drivers
1 set Phillips screw drivers
Large and small mole grip
Large and small pliers
Wire cutters
Hack saw
Heavy hammer
Rubber hammer
Allen keys
Feeler gauge
Metal chisel
Hand drill and bits
Plastic tubing (3 sizes)
Wire (high and low tension)
Some aluminium wire (hanger)
Pop rivet gun and rivets
Some piping

Small hydraulic jack
Releasing fluid
Grease
Jump leads
Set overalls
Sets of plastic gloves
Cleaning powder
Sand paper
Centre punch
Tool kit cases
Avo. (volt and amp meter)
Compression tester
Shifting spanner
Split pins, nuts, bolts etc

14. Skiddoo and Snowcat

One Snowcat fully equipped
Two skiddoos and trailers
Petrol containers for glacier
Food containers for glacier
Roof rack for Snowcat
SSB radio in Snowcat (single side band)
Ropes in case of dropped Snowcat in
    crevasse
Spades for igloo building
Trailer for skiddoo
Oil for skiddoo and Snowcat
Tool kit and spares
Generator
Trailers to be pulled by skiers

15. Food and Packaging

12 People for around 6 weeks

Stage 1 10 people 22nd – 26th July,
    Reykjavík
Stage 2 12 people 27th – 6th Aug, glacier
    (5 days spare)
Stage 3 12 people 7th – 15th Aug, river
    (rafts plus vehicles)
Stage 4 14 people 16th – 31st Aug, canyon
    section Dettifoss etc.
Each day's rations packed as 12-man day;
    plus a condiments box.
15 tea chests
10 fish barrels (waterproof)

16. Fuel and Containers

Fuel required for two vehicles, Snowcat, aircraft, microlights, skiddoos, generator, heating fuel, helicopter.

1800 litres, petrol
1200 litres, diesel
1000 litres, Augas
25 litres, pre-mix
25 litres, BP Coranda
10 litres, Varellus

Other Fuel
50 kg grill coal
20 litres special grill coal fuel
2 burners for gaz

17. Radio Equipment

Headsets for microlight pilots
VHF system for camera crew
VHF system for raft
VHF system for microlight pilots
Base station in vehicles

SSB set in Snowcat
SSB set to be used in vehicles

Spares
Batteries
Charger system
Spare fitting wires etc

18. Sail Boat

Boat fully equipped
Life jackets (see raft)
Outer protective garments
Helly Hansen inner

Foot wear (see wet suit stuff)
Whistles
Radio equipment
Food
Other equipment (kayaks, raft etc)

19. Specific Papers, Certificates, Maps etc.

Maps of all parts of route, covered in plastic sheet
Written permission from oil company (Olís) to obtain fuel in any garage
Team details (who to contact in case of accident, passport numbers)
Money
Address of sponsors for sending post cards from Reykjavík
Phone numbers of contacts in Iceland
Phone and telex numbers of contacts in France and Britain
Phone numbers of suppliers in Britain and France

20. Survival Aids

Some flares
Compass
Waterproof matches
Knives
Hyperthermia bags
Food rations
Water purifying tablets
Glacier cream
Water filter
Torches